T0195842

www.trafford.com
North America & international
toll-free: 844-688-6899 (USA & Canada)
fax: 812 355 4082

The Fool's Tarot

An Introduction to the Triune World
of the Three Arcana

Gerald-Johan Van Waes

The Fool's Tarot

An Introduction to the Triune World of the Three Arcana

Gerald-Johan Van Waes

Based upon seventy-eight cards from the Major and Minor Arcana
with the two additional positions "Truth" and "Intuition"
adopted and adapted from the book *The Complete New Tarot*
by Onno and Rob Docters van Leeuwen

Acknowledgements

My thanks to Ian Wanless and especially R. G. Theil for their valuable assistance in the early English drafts of this work, and also once more for the finalisation of its feedback process of editing path 29, the Overview of the Paths, and for editing appendix 3.

Appreciation is due to Brad Stewart at the Sacred Science Institute for his help and encouragement in bringing this work through to publication.

My sincerest gratitude to Brian McKillop for his editorial revisions and helpful suggestions.

Early developments of the deck dedicated to BA, who encouraged the need for such a work.

CONTENTS

And the way is to be ordinary—*then you become extraordinary; the way is to be just the last and then suddenly you find you are the first; the way is not to claim the credit and then nobody can take it from you; the way is to exist as a non-being, as a nobody, and then, in a subtle and mysterious way, you and only you become somebody—somebody the whole existence feels blessed with, feels blessed by, someone with whom the whole existence celebrates.*

—Osho

INTRODUCTION

In the majority of traditional approaches to the interpretation of tarot, familiarity with "the system" develops through a process of image association and symbol interpretation. As a result of this, the Reader is encouraged to adopt an *associative method* that largely focuses on images and symbols.[1] Whilst this legitimate interpretative endeavour may serve to extend the range of personal reflections, it nonetheless remains limited to the number and combination of associations the Reader has managed to assemble prior to the moment of interpretation. This factor permits a certain arbitrariness to creep into the interpretative process.

In the case of divination for others, whosoever subsequently listens to and follows these interpretations cannot say with much confidence what is fantasy and what is the result of associations linked to the internal psychology of the Reader. In short, the determining emphasis may prove in time to be little more than an expression of the Reader's own expectations. What is perhaps of greater concern in such scenarios is that the productive effects of these presuppositions may (and often do) begin to take on a life of their own as a result of the associative method. For this reason, at a certain point in one's progress with the tarot, the weaknesses in the associative method become burdensome and fail to assist one's further development.

It must never be forgotten that the essence of tarot work is directed towards *understanding*. It is the thesis of this work that such understanding can be structured much better than traditional methods allow when we adopt the perspective that the real essence of tarot is not to be captured through images alone. Anyone familiar with the basics of tarot theory will acknowledge the fact that certain methods of interpretation describe some cards as being "negative" and thereby encourage, knowingly or unknowingly, a moral perspective that implicitly suggests that the duty of interpretation is to indicate the path that will lead to the transformation of such negatives. In this work, however, each card is initially treated as being "neutral." This means that each card offers a situation (or event) that may evoke a heartfelt *emotional response*, a direct *instinctive response*, a *rational response*, or a response resulting from a *physical exchange*. As the Reader begins to experience these different orientations and how they serve to automatically generate an assortment of associations and combinations, as well as how they can be interpreted in their own context and reflected on, the Reader begins to realise his or her own place in the process of interpretation. The Reader then begins to discover another mode of conducting the process of interpretation and how to put this process to use in a more practical way.

Thus, in practicing the method of *The Fool's Tarot*, the Reader never considers the input of any given spread to be "good" or "bad" but instead simply views it as being a "fact-targeted" description, which, thanks to this new approach, can be explained and guided more carefully. It is also hoped that not only will the interpretations resulting from this new directive become more manageable—precisely because things will become much more recognisable—but also that the reader will come to a much deeper understanding that considers every situation as an event pertaining to the natural order of things.

So if the Reader would simply agree to begin again, to slowly approach the inner significance of the individual cards and try to comprehend the structure upon which each is built, he or she would soon come to realise the necessity of passing beyond the limitations of image formation and the arbitrariness of the associative field.

The Reader would then come to discover that the real essence of tarot is, beyond all psychic associations and astral excursions, something much more *dynamic*. Of course, not every Reader will

---

[1] The "Reader" with capital *R* refers to the interpreter of tarot cards.

find this deeper level so easy of access, and there will always be those who adamantly refuse to experiment and refine their methods of interpretation. Such persons will prefer instead to keep themselves and those they read for shackled to the whims of their own imagination. Again, there will be those who associate tarot with numerology and find their anchor in this and other so-called abstract notions. Here, again, we repeat that this work is not concerned with such secondary methods. In *The Fool's Tarot*, what matters from the outset is that the Reader learn to think in a more *vital* and less mechanical way. The advantage of this transition is that the Reader will soon find themselves opening up to an entirely different source of inspiration that operates not by association but through a vital logic of evolving patterns.

This shift from an associative logic to a more distinctly *intuitive approach* possesses its own rewards and requires of the serious Reader a certain capacity as well as the development of a particular skill. This skill, if properly mastered, leads the Reader to rediscover a tarot that no longer simply works with images but passes beyond them to make contact with other levels of consciousness. Thus, for those who wish to go further, we offer *The Fool's Tarot*, a work that has been created not just to counter the excessive use and abuse of astral incentives but also to initiate the serious Reader into the essential kernel of the Great Game.

Chapter 1 introduces us to the Major Arcana, or twenty-two fundamental stances. Presented in a story format, each card of the Major Arcana is understood as a preliminary phase in the learning process of a personality still dependent on the cycle of experience. Passing through the known order of the cards, intuitive logic begins to reveal the vital story of life, which connects the cards to their mythical origin and the deeper revelation of the phases of genesis. This profound pattern is also reflected in the process of human awakening. Each phase or card functions to stress an area of focus necessitating attention to make awareness of the greater process clear. If we understand human beings as always operating within the midst of a process of change, we will intuit the notion that our perception in each phase notices only one facet of the overall process. However, as *The Fool's Tarot* aims to reveal to understand the whole of the tarot teaching, one must learn to access each succeeding phase until the wholeness of the process within the part and the part within the process becomes clear. Only then can one put the teaching of *The Fool's Tarot* into practice and recognise (in advance) the rhythms of each phase in the cycle.

In chapters 2, 3, 4, and 5, we discover how the *primary experiences* of the Major Arcana are deepened through the developments of the Minor Arcana. Here, a shift in level occurs in which the personality learns to shape and form its sensed experiences via a learning process controlled by the four "bodies" or centres of experience. The author provides a thorough description of these different levels of experience, together with their patterns and learning processes. These pave the way for the later transition from the realm of experience to the realm of essences. Before this transition is possible, however, a means of coordination and integration is necessary. Chapter 6 explains how this may be achieved through the two additional cards "Truth" and "Intuition."[2]

Existing as "buffer zones" between the Major and Minor Arcana, these two cards operate as "anchor points," which assist the Reader's orientation within the phases of enfoldment. By incorporating the cards Truth and Intuition into his tarot spreads, the Reader is shown a method for filtering out fantasy and for advancing a more directed interpretation, which is able to assimilate the known while penetrating the "unknown."

---

[2] The adoption of the cards "Truth" and "Intuition" are adapted from the Tarot of the Restored Order.

Chapter 8 initiates us into the processes of recovery in both the Major and Minor Arcana. In chapter 9, we are introduced into the mysteries of the Third Arcana. Here, the central thesis of *The Fool's Tarot* becomes clear: The Major and Minor Arcana alone are an incomplete process. A Third Arcana is necessary to facilitate the process of self-recovery and restoration on all levels of being. The Reader who has understood the evolving patterns of events simultaneously on the four levels of experience passes naturally into this third phase of awareness. In this abstract field, the Reader's experiential understandings are finally able to float free from biases as the mind becomes unconstrained and opens up to engagement with the thirty-two intelligences, which correspond to the thirty-two Paths of Wisdom. Each new phase opened up evokes a specific mode of intelligence (or inspiration), which assists the reader in redressing the adverse effects resulting from earlier incomplete phases of experience related to the previous Arcana. Step by step, then, the author invites us to explore the dynamic relationships of the "Grand Scheme," which is perhaps the most comprehensive mandala ever produced on the tarot.

But for whom is this Grand Scheme devised, and *who* will walk this path? The answer is to be found in the title. *The Fool's Tarot* disavows the conventional identification of the Reader with the figure of the Magician and replaces it with that of the Fool. As Gurdjieff's "Toast to the Idiots" sought to remind his followers: *Are provisions not being made for fools at all times and everywhere?*[3]

What, then, are the possibilities for a fool in each phase of the Third Arcana? To answer this question, the Reader must first discover what the danger of maintaining a rigid attitude may mean for each subsequent phase in the journey. Everything must be lived and vitally experienced on this path. Everything must be incorporated and all suggestions digested. Since there exists such diversity among fools, there will be various kinds of rhythms and different degrees of emphasis. If the fool in his folly cannot make the choice that will bring him improvement, then the lowest level of the random event (as we find it expressed in the Major Arcana) will dominate. Then it will be Dame Nature herself who will don the mask of the Fool, while man merely dreams of being a Magician.

To begin, then, let us take a walk through the cards one by one, adopting the open and flexible attitude of the Fool, who knows nothing. Let us venture along this path and assume—if assume we must—only one thing: that each card is but one aspect or phase in a learning process, which, step by step, leads us gradually and necessarily to the perception of the abstract nature of the whole.

---

[3] Among his teaching methods, Gurdjieff used a ritual he called "Toasts to the Idiots." The "toast" in question was not meant in any pejorative sense; the Latin *idiota* is derived from Greek and refers to one's own, private, peculiar. Gurdjieff had a scale of twenty-one "idiots" based on increasing levels of spiritual attainment, and not on individual peculiarities. The "Toasts to the Idiots" was aimed at highlighting and eventually breaking forms of crystallized self-knowledge rather than indicating any individual characteristic.

1

THE MAJOR ARCANA

Welcome, Reader. You have donned your feathered cap and are now a Major Fool. Does this alarm you? If so . . . well . . . this is as it should be . . . thither the tinkle of Jester's bells . . . If not . . . beware!

We shall begin our journey with the twenty-two cards of the Major Arcana, which, from now on, we will refer to simply as the twenty-two *fundamental stances*. By this word "stance," we mean at one and the same time a basic attitude/a posture/a behaviour/a position.[4] The twenty-two general stances can be thought of as types of attitude we display in life or towards other people. They indicate how and where we stand in relation to situations or events at a given time and are usually assumed in an *automatic* or mechanical way.

As we proceed along the path of the cards, these stances become mobilised. With each step taken, new "strengths" are acquired or, perhaps more accurately, new *emphases* are stressed. None of the steps reached are superior to any of the others. Each step taken presents new "disadvantages," so that one becomes increasingly aware of the necessity to maintain the momentum of the whole. All such "disadvantages" are actually only the residues of impossibilities that automatically arrange themselves against the potentialities of the next phase. The sooner one realises that this situation indicates a *double potential*, the sooner one learns to evaluate the nature of one's present attitude or choice.

---

[4] Besides indicating a posture adopted in standing, the English word "stance" also refers to a point of view or attitude taken. It also has the additional meaning of a place where mountain climbers may belay. The Latin root of this word, which is still retained to this day in Italian, is *stanza*, referring to a stopping place or station.

(1)

The first and most easily adopted stance is that of consciously acknowledging who and where you are right now in the present moment. This is the experience of one's own force field, one's own patterns, and one's own power of projection. This stance is perceived as possessing a divine core or "nucleus" around which is formed the world as its shadow. This centre senses its own origins and looks for like-minded people and results that can confirm this origin. It is the centralisation of one's own thought and the strength to realise it. When finding success through the coincidence of kinship, this double-energy creates "magic," performing wonders by "playing the magician." If, however, one encounters persons very differently disposed to oneself, one seems unable to achieve much from this stance or viewpoint.

The arrow in the above drawing shows the direction of this masculine phallic-like energy, an expanding force radiating outwards and upwards from a single centre. One's personal faith is, in one sense, a projection of one's overall effectiveness. If one really deals only with the known thought processes issuing from oneself, little appears to go awry.

(2)

The Priestess looks beyond the Magician because she realises for the first time the *other-ness* of others. By doing so, she learns to pay attention to the contradictions that apparently exist between the inner and the outer world. She looks within to consult with her internal states and expresses these to the outside. Her energy is feminine.

The Priestess works with all the contradictions we meet seeking to form them into a functional whole. In this stance, the potential power of things is discovered and with experience increased in volume. Yet not all contradictions confronted here are considered as constituting workable material (or possessing potential). Only what is brewing for cooperation is considered workable.

(3)

The third attitude relates to a search for further applications of what is deemed productive to gain additional results. Since this is the first awareness of a world acting on its own outside oneself, this power is called the Empress. Its posture is still feminine, yet it now realises very well the differences between inner world and the outer world applications and has the desire to expand the relationship between them.

(4)

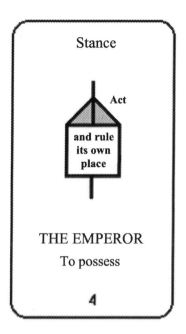

The fourth stance benefits from the acquisition, discovery, and rearrangement of contradictions by means of which one masters and acquires a place of one's own—the things that can be handled—in such a way as to achieve an attitude of self-assuredness. From here, this attitude has enough power to act and to produce real accomplishments. Hence, this card is also called the Emperor or Ruler. This ruler is in control and possesses a secure position from which to act.

(5)

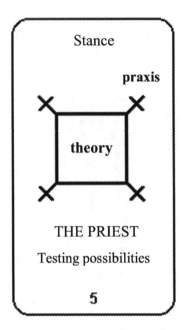

When the "acting" leads to habit formation and obtains thereby a sense of security, the time has come to develop praxis. This can proceed through balanced reason and will be elaborated initially via theory. The practice itself or how the action will be achieved through practice remains the testing ground for this person who is often presented in the role of teacher, priest, or hierophant.

(6)

Stance

THE LOVER

Power of exchange

6

Having managed to evaluate the complete working area, one now knows it is possible within this area to achieve something of a practical nature. Things succeed now in an optimal way because we begin to realise that the "other" is best recognised as someone with the same range of capacities as ourselves. The attitude of the Lover is in fact the possibility of an exchange principle, which can act for one or against whatever one opposes. Being a more advanced working area, this exchange force can bring joy when it functions well, as, for example, in the case of "lovers."

(7)

Once one is able to perceive the experiential fullness that the principle of exchange is able to bring about, an appearance of expertise is produced and a sense of knowing what one is dealing with. This increases one's awareness and bestows an attitude of confidence in relation to how one handles things. This stage is called Carriage or, in the terminology of the traditional tarot, the Chariot. What one learns here possesses a certain richness, a knowledge that is not the result of having been taught something but a manifestation of tried-and-tested experience. Thus, with this quality, one obtains a certain personality or personal style with which to handle one's affairs. In other words, what is learned through the process of exchange is now dealt with in a personalised way.

(8)

One can benefit from the success of one's own manifestation in such a way that one will expand through it. The attitude of this card gives shape to this kind of *qualitative exaltation*—strengthening one's own strength—which may also be translated as lust and often expressed as macho-ness or sexiness. In any case, this approach aims to assemble results through its own manifestation. It refers to an *excess of energy,* which can be exuded as something "extra."

(9)

Stance

THE HERMIT

Extending
through/from
one's own power

9

In the focused awareness of one's own potential irradiation, one can also adopt the quiet controlled attitude of someone who does not need to prove himself or herself anymore.

This is the card of the Hermit. From here, one examines how balance can be rediscovered through what has already been created. The card does not suggest that this is already a realisation but rather that there comes a moment in one's life where it is necessary to adopt an attitude that avails of the opportunity to restore order and balance. In fact, this attitude comes as the acknowledgement of a duty or personal task.

(10)

Stance

WHEEL OF FORTUNE

Chance
in all possible
extensions

10

Whatever further extensions are undertaken hereafter remains dependent on chance circumstances. At this stage, one recognises that it is not necessary to give primacy at all costs to one's own achievements. Although one is no longer wholly dependent on one's capacity for performance, the possibility for further achievements continues to be bound to "chance." This sort of chance is called the Wheel of Fortune, also known as *The Wheel of Destiny*.[5]

One looks forward to one's fortune in a state of expectancy because what is to come is still a completely unknown area and the sum total of options lies beyond one's control. This *unknown factor* is accepted without fear and with openness precisely because only this attitude allows all possibilities to happen. The condition of leaving it open to chance is necessary because one understands that one really has no personal control over it. At the same time, one has no real responsibility for it either since all experiences are considered to be only the consequences of a journey and nothing more.

The real "other-ness" now appeals as the sum total of all new possibilities. During the process of discovery affecting one's personal fate, there is a sense one does not need to integrate every encounter. One has now the advantage of adopting an attitude, which is not obliged to seek any achievement for oneself. Gradually, one learns *discernment* and how to "place" every encounter. So long as one lets everything pass without judgement, the wheel of fortune keeps running in the same vein.

---

[5] The circle in the drawing of the Wheel of Fortune can express the personality that, like a lemniscate (∞), is on a turning point about to take a new way. Which way the personality turns still depends on chance. The final choices that will be taken are already lying beyond the choices coming from the limitations of the constructed personality alone.

(11)

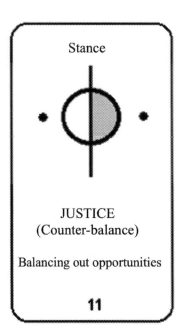

Stance

JUSTICE
(Counter-balance)

Balancing out opportunities

11

At a certain moment, there comes the opportunity to seize some of the more frequently occurring results derived through chance. By means of a certain degree of control, one manages to balance out these opportunities in which both talents and shortcomings are able to survive. It is this kind of counterbalancing of capabilities/opportunities that constitutes true justice in any judgement. This is not about envisioning the "right situation" but about adopting an attitude that is able to provide the right understanding of what factors are lurking behind situations. Balancing a set of presenting elements in casual situations requires a special kind of talent, a talent that could be best described by this attitude.

(12)

It is common for people to continue to judge what is valuable or not valuable to them based on the development of personal experiences, which still remain limited by chance. The personality, apparently right and with an idiosyncratic logic of its own, develops an attitude of sustained stubbornness and maintains a desire to continue on its way even though it may be woefully out of balance with the whole development of things themselves. This is the reason why at some stage a confrontation becomes apparent and eventually clarifies the contradictions being produced in this way.

This sort of situation forces the person(ality) to alter its stance. The attitude of this card we call the Hanged Man, which traditionally represents a man hanging upside down. His head is where his feet should be, and his feet are where his head should be. Another way of saying this is *he has lost control of the ground beneath his feet.*

As a matter of fact, this is a good thing as this situation forces one to revise the general vision one has constructed up until this point. The opportunity for adjustment and reversal happens through conditions provided outside of oneself. This situation can also be followed *consciously* by adjusting one's ideas and overall vision and aligning them with this newly presented reality. In ancient rituals, the hanged man was hung from a tree. All impractical, dualistic, and disconnected ways of thinking were thus brought back into natural balance through the vital organic rhythms of the tree.

(13)

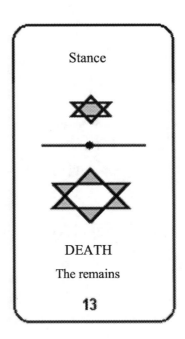

What emerges from the residues of the former experience reveals itself automatically through the whole situation that now transpires. The attitude adopted in relation to this "surplus" (or remains) is called Death because one distances oneself from this thing that one no longer needs or that is no longer needed in this form. At this point of "death," the essential essence, which is leftover, is self-limiting. Discovering what still remains as "leftover" is the unknown area proposed by this card.

(14)

Now that one is able to maintain a distance from all that has been achieved, one is able to take a distinctly more moderate attitude towards all that had to be left behind. One is also better equipped to evaluate what remains at a distance and to counterbalance elements for the benefit of harmony. If this was simply a question of formal aspects alone, one would call this balancing of the elements *aesthetics*. In general, however, it is a creative view and treatment. Accordingly, to function properly, it requires a certain method of blending elements with one another. The essence of this act(ivity) is "Art." One might also compare it with cooking in the sense that this, too, is an activity, which requires the correct proportions of elements blended with each other to make a satisfactory whole.

How effective these results will be in the end is the unknown factor in this stance. One has undertaken this path towards results with the intention of making things more beautiful. Through the experience of the previous stance, one has learned that personal desire alone attends the risk of losing the results completely. Hence, this mode of construction is now done more cautiously. One deals circumspectly with the issues that will be presented. Here, one also develops something with elements that do not "belong" to oneself. By adopting an attitude that maintains a certain distance from such issues allows one to tap and further develop their potential. Nevertheless, one will have no idea as to the effect these results will have on others or even how others will react to this emerging talent.

(15)

Stance

THE DEVIL

The shadow side
of one's power
begins to emerge

15

It may happen that the right effect was not produced in the things we created and organised in terms of what we initially had in mind when we began the process. Something completely different may occur than what was expected. Moreover, the proposed effect may fail to be progressive for the whole. In the long run, this means it may not be progressive for oneself or others despite our original intention to benefit all. It may be the case that our objective was to try to deal as best we could with everything we were aware of at that particular time. However, having taken a particular perspective or formed a particular opinion about things, one has neglected something else (to one's disadvantage) and caused a curtailment of energies, which has now locked up potential capacities in a certain self-defeating imprisonment from which one cannot now escape.

The stance of the Devil is the attitude we take when facing squarely the *shadow side* of our own creations, which, because of our stubborn tendency to proceed with something at any cost, exposes our limitations.

The unknown territory in this stance is not knowing how one's deeds or the actions one has initiated in the past manage to achieve something constructive over time. This tendency for constructive renewal exists within circumstances in which there cannot be any clear predictability. What one learns to understand here is the nature and character of drawbacks that exist within one's own creative formats and the kind of consequences that may result from our modes of approach. To recognise such issues and to face them squarely allows for the confrontation that permits us to see the "mask of the maker." One should be able to recognise the maker's effectivity and in this way learn what produces the most direct effects in certain types of creations. What direction such effects will later take is again unknown territory.

(16)

Stance

THE FALLING TOWER

A test case for
one's commitment

16

The next card, the (Falling) Tower, brings clarity to the uncertainty concerning long-term effects. The results obtained by the Tower depend on the kind of energy one has put into things. In this stance, the personality that has "done the creating" comes last. It is now seen as the ivory tower from which an aspect of reality has escaped.

In the renewed attitude that comes with the Tower, one becomes aware of the core or origin of one's own energy, which in the long term will be able to attract and accumulate corresponding energies. However, it will not necessarily be the case that the like-minded will gravitate to you and the differently minded will be kept at a distance—a wish that the last card still hoped for.

What this stance indicates is that one will literally and very definitely reap what one attracts *as well as* what one repels. This situation occurs in the middle of a test or trial with which one must be actively engaged. In general, the question that resounds at this juncture is this: *Is the kind of energy presently being put into something really the correct one?* One who now senses how best to use this energy in a more responsive way is turning this area to his or her advantage.

(17)

To gain more insight into what makes sense in the long term, one can no longer leave the effects of creations as they are—something that one still did at the position of the card the Devil. Nor can one any longer continue to think that the right mentality will be sufficient to gain the appropriate results—according to the acquisitions of the previous card—by simply adopting the stance of "the Tower." Rather, to obtain the necessary overview, one now realises it is better to test the plans themselves as well as their direct effects in the long term by checking the present possibilities with which one could or would want to plan something. Only then will the uncertainty effect present a sensible perspective—that is to say, present a sense that actually exists or that is at least imaginable. When converting this into practice, one has to be especially vigilant. This "stellar attention" is the *test area* pertaining to this stance.

In the above card, you can see how the symbol or pattern of the activity (the six-pointed star) emerges to fit the larger pattern (the seven-pointed star). The *waves of water* in the design become here a symbol of the pattern of a life course.

(18)

Stance

THE MOON

Flood of Feeling

18

In the fullness of realisations, one can now express one's own expectations and desires and articulate or project these onto the world. The card that expresses this is the Moon. Because this energy is *expanding*, the Moon can easily be associated with an extension or increase of feeling(s). The mental aspect of this extension, however, cannot be followed by the ordinary way of thinking and can in fact only be stimulated through and after the recognition of its mystical character. This energy of "full expectation" radiates so fully and freely that it has a powerful impact on the environment and automatically opens up unknown pathways. From this stance, one observes a more naturally fruitful environment than is normally seen from the ordinary perspective. What is required of one here is to simply be the conduit for the Moon's causal flux to enable its extension to bring about its effects. In the Crowley deck, this card is expressed by the scarabeus, a symbol used as a lucky charm that works on the rhythm of something much greater than oneself as, for example, on the rhythmic rising and descending of the sun. Something of the scarab's deeper symbolism is revealed by Isha Schwaller de Lubicz when she tells us, "The scarab symbolises the principle of *the being who realises through himself the elements of his own becoming and transformation.*"[6]

For those who remain dependent on the motive or on the source of their creation, the changes experienced in this stage evoke a mixture of feelings from deep-seated scepticism to cautiousness and anxiety because the evolution here inaugurated is towards something that is no longer in their own hands. The unknown here is just *how* or *where* the good occasions remain in existence. This "open environment" is the learning process deeply felt and experienced in the reign of influence of the Moon.

To experience a lasting liberation of this energy, it is best not to admire or worship the causal aspect of its flux because of the danger of falling victim to a reliance upon it. This said, the admiring receiver cannot be anything other than an energy propagation.

---

[6] Isha Schwaller de Lubicz, *Her-Bak: Egyptian Initiate*, p. 296 (Inner Traditions 1978).

When one learns to see its existence as pure causality alone, then one comes to understand that there are so many causal forces that may, in their turn, be able to increase and propagate further aspects of the same energy. This latter realisation is an additional bounty that can be learned from this card.

(19)

In the previous phase, the Moon recognised a form of increase *in and from itself*. Having now become aware of this energy and familiar with its deeper essence, one can learn to identify oneself with this burgeoning process. In this way, one is able to become the broker of this energy, and because of this, a different expression of it will become more appropriate—namely, that of the Sun. The stance adopted here is that of reducing oneself to the *essence* of one's own propagative power and learning to irradiate this essence further and apply it to the known that propagates itself. In the Rider-Waite deck, this essence is depicted as a child on top of a horse. Of course, the "child" in question is no naive babe-in-the-wood but an entity who is innocently open to the world and its essentials, experiencing all and everything as though it were forever new.

(20)

Stance

JUDGEMENT

Re-use

20

The attitude of the (Final) Judgement occurs at a moment when one is finally ready to exist simply as essence and to irradiate this essence with a readiness to sacrifice it when necessary.

In fact, it is quite normal at this stage to find oneself in a totally different world from the one that one had hitherto been used to. This "difference" consists in an openness to what is a completely new cycle of opportunities, some of which may involve repetitions, whilst others demand a willingness to sacrifice something for an opportunity—which at this stage will amount to a major change. The extent to which one opens up attitudinally will lead to a different way of organising some of the contradictions in the outer world and thereby determine the degree of innovation permitted in the new cycle. The degree to which one renews or repeats oneself in circumstances is the test ground for the Judgement.

On the drawing for this card, the circles represent two summaries of "life course'" within an environment of applications. A certain degree of change in one life course may alter this whole and lead it to assume a proportionately different form.

(21)

Via this new enfoldment of essence, one can now imagine one's own place in the Universe because one now knows it. In fact, in this phase, one looks to one's creative possibilities through the adoption of a certain (selected) life purpose. One creates an image of a particular option or possibility, but the real secret of this stage is to review again all one's existing possibilities. To uncover these possibilities is the unknown component of this card.

Simply put: at this juncture, one looks for one's own place in the world.

(22)

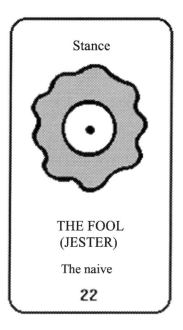

Stance

THE FOOL
(JESTER)

The naive

22

Rather than imagine what one could achieve in life, one can instead—whilst not wishing to instil any preconceptions—opt to omit such imagining and remain completely open to all that is happening around one. This kind of attitude, through which one remains in touch with one's true *intuition*, is called the Fool (the Jester or Joker). This attitude does not necessarily seek to prove itself directly and may indeed only be working out a plan for this later. In the meantime, the Fool is thoroughly himself wherever he is, free from the advantages or disadvantages of long-term plans, which only result in the development of complex contradictions by way of the results of the other twenty-one cards. The unknown territory here is everything but unconsciousness.

The advantage of adopting the stance of the Fool is that it will not provoke any conflicts or contradictions through the limitations of a particular perspective or talent. Even though a talent or visualisation could easily develop by undertaking a course of action, the Fool continues to exist unmoved by the pull of such momentum, preferring instead to remain steadfastly removed from the strictures of such cycles. In the phase of the Fool, therefore, one is open to fundamental change or to a different order of contradictions from those one was previously used to, and, at the same time, one also remains in a state of limbo adopting the adage "live and let live." The unknown terrain here concerns the question of how one might become conscious of the quality of this freedom.

It is to the Minor Arcana we will now turn to answer this question.

THE MINOR ARCANA

2

HEARTS / CUPS
TRIALS BY WATER

The heart differentiates itself by opening itself for a direct effect.

Besides adopting this or that general stance towards the world and outer events, it is also possible that certain areas of experience may come to dominate. Take, for example, the area of *feelings*. It is our feelings that colour our basic attitudes with various qualities such as those of warmth, affection, and so on. Furthermore, in the realm of feelings, we come to experience "different phases of the unknown," which progress by degrees of refinement up until the point where the experience of feelings become so full and complete that they become entirely known to us, so much so in fact that they enable us to embrace more fully the unfamiliar in ourselves.

(1)

The Queen of Hearts or Cups is the first card in this series that contains the complete potential and full possibility of feelings. In *The Fool's Tarot*, the Queen of Hearts refers to the importance of the "pounding of the heart," which will enable the core or essence to spread its effect outwardly.

(2)

Hearts ♡ Cups

THE KING

Directed feelings:
Desire

2nd step: "in volume"

At the stage where all the potential in the life of feelings has discovered a place to go to, it receives there a causal impulse capable of taking its radiance in the direction of its target. One could call this *directed energy* "desire." In the above card, it is connected with the third point of the heart. The power to achieve one's goal passes through it in a distinctly masculine way. Therefore, this card is represented by the King. The results, which the target will deliver, remain unknown, whilst the feeling for what is desired is familiar.

(3)

Hearts ♡ Cups

THE KNIGHT

The Totality
of feelings:
Locomotion

3rd step: whole

As soon as the target is fully known and the movements in the heart become complete and receive a place to go to, they can then proceed in a conscious direction. The unknown territory here concerns the question of what this totality may be able to accomplish in real life. This card is called the Knight because it is here that the *undertaking* prevails.

(4)

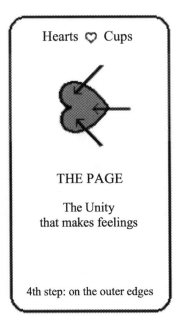

The next card is called the Page or Princess. Here, the undertaking is less important than what is emitted. Something now begins to radiate from the Page. Even though the life path has now developed, a clarifying form the unknown terrain concerns the issue of *where* the feelings will come to belong. Consider the story of the princess in the fairy tale who tests the incoming princes and, in this way, takes them into account. Following the initial recognition, there exists a connection between what will be accomplished on the life path and the effect it will have on the functioning of the heart. Opening up to a phase of testing prevails here.

(5)

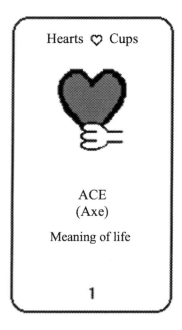

Hearts ♡ Cups

ACE
(Axe)

Meaning of life

1

When one fully comprehends the assignment of the previous card—which reveals a unity of feelings in which there exists a pure form of giving and receiving—room is made available for an interaction between the feelings of the heart and some new incentives. This card is called Ace (or Axe). Emerging from the sum total of interactions taken into account, one now feels strong enough to pour out the content of one's conscious life in a more concrete form. The feelings known in this way now have the possibility of being expressed directly. The impact of this new totality is the unknown terrain here. Its experiences are now located in its most viable life-giving field of expression.

(6)

Through the expression of feelings, one comes to realise that this also means the sharing of feelings. The interaction that occurs here causes the heart to beat differently because it is now fed from two sources as, for example, in the case of two people who become attached through a given destiny. This card is called Love because the love between two people works in this way: becoming strong through an interaction of life energy and purposefulness—although this card need not necessarily refer to a love affair.

(7)

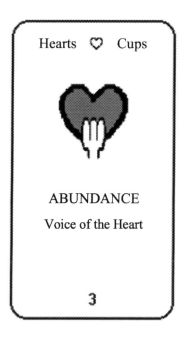

Hearts ♡ Cups

ABUNDANCE

Voice of the Heart

3

As soon as one begins to grasp the interactions taking place between the feelings present, one starts to attribute a personal value to them. This card marks the stage of Abundance. Here, the hand in the card "handles" the third target point—that is, the foundation, which keeps the heart going. One might also call this procreation—the formation of *the voice of the heart*. The objectives one begins to handle during this activity now constitute the new working area, which challenges the heart's proper efficacy. Here, one expresses the desire to intensify and amplify this inner strength. One cannot know for sure what the effect of increasing the heart's inner motives will be because that is the unknown territory of this card. Additional attributes of the heart's motivation may be compassion, sympathy, or even antipathy. The addition of these characteristics gives such feelings a purpose. In effect, the *voice of the heart* expresses all that is dear or closest to one's heart.

(8)

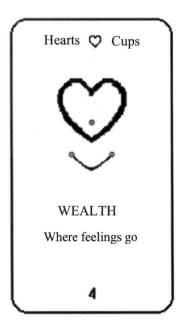

If one knows the likely effects of one's motives on another person, one can open up to that other person and formulate plans with the aggregate of these feelings. Such plans are often made in line with what one feels and with what relates to oneself. One explores what these results might offer and then daydreams about their possibilities. In reality, what the final effect will be and what this might mean for the other person remains unknown because up until now, one has not really taken into account the feelings of the other. Even though these motives are in essence the beating of a heart, they cannot predict or determine where each heart is really going. What one notices here are the possibilities of certain further connections between unknown features as they continue to flow into an unfamiliar whole. Hence, it often feels as though one is taking a risk and proceeding into the unknown. Here, one prepares oneself for additional options that lie outside of one's control.

(9)

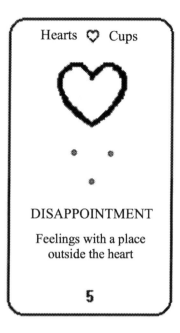

Hearts ♡ Cups

DISAPPOINTMENT

Feelings with a place
outside the heart

5

Many of the possibilities of the pounding heart could go in any direction. However, they will not oppose reality for failing to find a suitable target or appropriate accord. One could say that the assumptions—or the proposed pounding from the other side—were too identified with one's own goals. Yet these assumptions lie completely *outside* the heart's real opportunities. Ultimately, the heart no longer has a place to go to. This can be interpreted as a recognition of how one's finite goals often seem empty. Often, this perception or recognition is accompanied by feelings of "disappointment." At the same time, it can also suggest an understanding that feelings have no fixed place within the heart. The unknown territory here is where feelings match. From desires and urges alone, one does not obtain this kind of vitality. Such vitality lies in the exploration of the unknown territory of this card.

When one understands this phase properly and recognises its appearance, one can keep oneself calm and detached in such a way that what has the vitality gets exactly what it is supposed to get and expresses that moment.

(10)

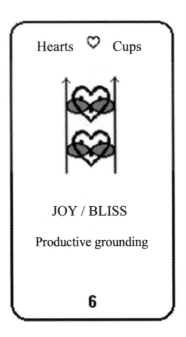

There comes a stage where the heart is driven forth on its own without need of any additional objective—which stands for the first type of beat—or without need of an extra boost to make the heart beat faster, as in the third beat. The heart gains volume and size—a second type of beat—knowing now how to find its own responsive place (thanks in large part to the direct effects that bring Joy). This type of joyful pleasure possesses a kind of naturalness and spontaneity without having to "mean" anything. The heart simply surrenders to all the things that bring joy.

The uncharted territory here is the new world that brings this joy. Such joy is, by itself, a force that is beyond the influence of individual feelings of motivation and, as such, is its own strength. The learning process that can occur here is one in which the previous motives are steered from the past and form their own kind of automated results according to aspects that may be either a stimulation or a discouragement according to the nature of the attraction. Yet this sense of being driven to the place of joy/bliss spontaneously forms itself into a power beyond goal projection and corresponding motives and thereby accumulates.

In the depiction of this card, you can see two sorts of drives or motives being stimulated by the volume that, like a surplus of naturally produced power, lies between the three aforementioned points of the heart. This vital energy is self-evident and arises from the source in which one lives and has one's being—a place in which none of the three types of direct motives are predominating. Here, then, between the three types of drives, we have nothing but a fully channelled energy that carries one to somewhere or to someone else. Only the strength of the flow towards the other, stimulated or inhibited from the past or in the present, measures the extent of how successfully this energy flows.

(11)

Responding only to what brings immediate joy does not provide any sense of liberation. Thus, one soon becomes dissatisfied with it. The overall effect of losing oneself in all that one designates as pleasure brings one to the phase of "corruption." If one allows for increasing expansion through one's feelings and sensitivity, the result in the end is that one loses control over where one's feelings go. Subsequently, one begins to lose this vital energy, which starts to flow towards things automatically. These new "places of feeling" no longer truly belong to the expansion of oneself but begin to gain a life of their own.

At this point, these magnified feelings are no longer in one's possession, and thus there results what one can label "sin." In Dutch, the word "sin" can also mean "pity," as in something shameful. More correctly, the word signifies a "wasteful misdirection of energy" because the energy in question no longer goes to the place where it can be properly effective. When this is the case, one knows only too well that one is no longer properly engaged. How to deal with this personal loss is the unknown terrain of this stage.

(12)

After a while, one knows what leads to certain favourable outcomes and what most certainly does not. It doesn't matter about the expression of those feelings when one is attempting to gauge where one has lost one's direction. Here, one needs to let go a bit, lick one's wounds, and carry on with what remains. What continues to provide further direction is everything that is tolerable and tolerant. What life now brings is some unknown abilities. In fact, here, one is no longer dependent on things that are not good for one. Yet the effect still lingers on. What one continues to accept and bear further is the unknown territory of this card.

An advantage of this phase is that one begins to project and extend further the centre of neutralisation in the heart—that is to say, that aspect that is most naturally present. It is a deep commitment to put the entire balance of sorrow and joy into life.

(13)

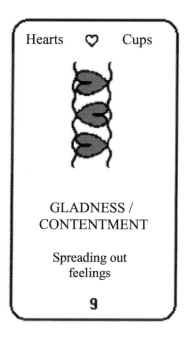

Hearts ♡ Cups

GLADNESS /
CONTENTMENT

Spreading out
feelings

9

As soon as one has taken the time to assemble all one's feelings, there comes the moment of enjoyment, a moment when one may propagate a sense of "gladness" or "contentment." In any case, the full sum of what one feels is here projected onto the life path and no longer onto personal goals. Seeking certain selective effects is no longer so important. The fact that something simply has its effect is viewed as perfectly natural. Learning how to deal with the totality of feelings in all situations with all their possibilities is the unknown territory of this phase.

(14)

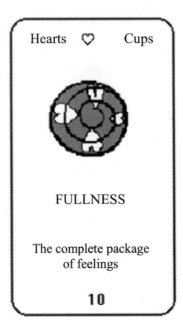

Hearts ♡ Cups

FULLNESS

The complete package
of feelings

10

As soon as one is able to apply the totality and vitality of feelings anywhere and at any time, one has mastered emotional self-control.

This stage of emotional wholeness represents the emotionally open person whom one intuitively feels is simply what he or she is. Such a person has accepted the full effect of the entire sum of their feelings. The unknown terrain for such a person is *everything*, and that is freedom.

3

DIAMONDS/WANDS/
TRIALS BY FIRE

Harsh and direct confrontations with reality: these we call Trials by Fire

The aforementioned reality in which "everything (simply) happens" is, of course, difficult to picture in the imagination since it remains subject to an idealised projection of feelings. Indeed, if an ideal response to this state really existed, would it not partake solely of the coloration of one's preferences? Would one not remain naïve and dependent on positive results with a constant need for circumstantial confirmation, which would provide the assurance that one can be accepted and can also accept anything anywhere? Necessarily, then, an area exists that presents *directly* all the different types of conditions of reality and their contradictions. This more extensive working area is represented by the suit of Diamonds or Wands.

The choice of the English word "diamond" for this particular suit is peculiar in that it does not really describe its real form, which is, in fact, a *rhombus*. Nevertheless, the choice of "diamonds" is still correct since diamonds are the hardest materials able to emerge from a fire process inside the earth. The Dutch word in this case refers more directly to the rhombus and indicates a field that is ploughed by men who work in it. In Flemish, the rhombus form is called *koeken* (or cookies), again because of its form, which represents an object to be consumed following a process of baking in an oven. In each of these symbolic associations, the reference is not aimed at the natural element of fire but rather to a working force that needs fire or pressure—some sort of dedicated and concentrated energy—for its expression. It is in this way that we must come to understand the different symbols associated with this suit. It would be wrong and misleading to associate this section solely with the notion of fire. The shape of the rhombus also suggests a kind of energetic matrix or environment in which a person dwells. With this in mind, it is worth mentioning at this moment that it is more practical to focus directly on the energy results themselves rather than on what lies in this region of perception.

The traditional tarot sign for this suit is, of course, the Wand or Fire Staff. This image of the magical staff refers to the conduction and projection of a type of electricity or lightning bolt and indicates the channelling of a natural electromagnetic force that exists between people. This force or energy expresses itself through the general state of tension present in situations and *not* with some direct or specific form of energy. Therefore, it is best viewed as an "intermediary flux," which is activated by action and reaction. In short, it is the *sum of all present energies*. The form it takes differs depending on the context, thus it may manifest as electricity, warmth, fire, or some other representative material. Crucially, this energy refers to the tactical positioning between the different elements involved and how they are directed through an innate instinctive behaviourism.

In the above drawing, the S rune-like bar or lightning bolt erupts from or strikes into the centre of the rhombus/diamond. The energy current—referring to a given situation or event—can be conceived as serving to receive a purpose or a directive. This energy current has three important and distinctive aspects: first, the commencement of the "fire," which is a direct confrontation not unlike an *inflammation*. This is followed by the *scalding* of the fire, which is the middle slash on our diagram. And, finally, there is the *receiving of the fire* or the result of it. The working area in this case is oriented in terms of *confrontation* and is the region of action and reaction.

To deal effectively with this kind of "energy," one must adopt different stances in relation to it. One might suppose that this working area would be easier to master once the mental faculties (Swords/Spades) have been sufficiently trained to receive it. Yet this suit or series of cards has been proposed at this point—following the phases of the heart—to show how confrontations emerge and how one can learn to navigate this working area with the proper attitudes. Merely rationalising the processes pertaining to these ongoing confrontations (which are extremely direct) would only be counterproductive in terms of aiding a breakthrough to grasping the valuable results of actions and reactions. Hence, this series is about getting to grips with immediate and inevitable confrontations by means of which one learns to estimate the true value of these phases.

When faced with this *direct energy*, it may happen that the confrontations encountered have a deleterious effect on one's ability to release or launch the totality of one's energy into the life stream. It may help to visualise the release of this direct energy in the form of an unfolding snake, similar in a sense to the Kundalini fire snake of the Eastern traditions. The sharp S form—compare again the S-shaped rune energy outlined above—and the rhombus on which it is oriented are the structure of the energy in focus. Through this, it will shape itself and be shaped.

(1)

Just as it was before in the previous suit, the first card of this series is the Queen phase. In this stance, it is the Queen who receives the energy from the base and checks the work area that arises from it. She, thus, has within her hands the emerging power of an area of action and reaction. She does not consider the consequences of this power but simply focuses on the pure raw energy of its creation. From her particular vantage point, the Queen is able to investigate what is most effective and of immediate consequence. The unknown area here concerns determining the degree of impact of one's activities.

Consider here the kind of leadership that has the capacity to remain level-headed in a position of responsibility for an area in which may occur many incalculable afflictions and trials.

When one conceives of this fire wand as the *unfolding* and *formation* of a "personality" (snake), one ought to take care and note at this stage whether the vital moment of its first "uncoiling" has sufficient elementary power for such a foundation. Controlling this unfolding of energy into the arena is best done with the proper foundation. If such a foundation exists, the energy may obtain there the employment of its action even though it will not yet be able to grasp where this is going to. Where the snake is catering for a new base or working area, the synthesis of its work should be sufficient to establish something to proceed with.

(2)

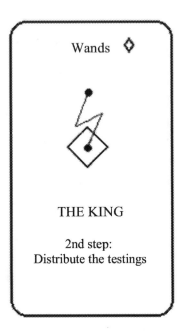

Wands ◊

THE KING

2nd step:
Distribute the testings

Having arrived in the middle of certain "activities" and having surveyed the response patterns, one now takes a more nuanced stance in the form of the King of Wands.

In the midst of one's own power, as both perpetrator and idealiser, one is able to notice that different types of situations lead to different kinds of actions and reactions. In fact, these ordeals will exist for one not at the centre of one's own personal task (where will and purpose are able to perish) but where the consequences of the manner in which one handles things will carry weight as an influence. Here, to minimise the negative impact, this new attitude or stance of the King will formulate a "division of tasks" in the form of assignments for his own benefit. This form of planning is a mode of preparation in which all kinds of unfortunate circumstances can be resolved and plans eventually succeed the better to guide further the final confrontations.

It is thanks to this division of labour that these assignments can lead to more viable confrontations with a minimum of action and reaction. One lays down in advance, so to speak, a constructive path to achieve something because a more straightforward approach will not obtain the desired results. Here, in fact, it is especially the province of the Prince as would-be King to prove that he is strong as a result of these commissions. This is not guided by the fundaments of "proving oneself" that occurs during a maturation process. Yet it is sufficient for defending oneself in small tasks in which the aim is to prove that one's place is legal even though the preconditions for one's presence might not always be so favourable. At first sight, the really favourable conditions for the Prince are not taken for granted as self-evident. In this way, he proves through a gradual process of realisation his right to be worthy of the reality of this place.

To better understand the above, recall if you will the fairy tales in which a prince is the recipient of certain commands, which he must fulfil before being able to attain the woman of his dreams. Consider again those tales in which the King who is issuing these commands wants to ensure that he who succeeds him will not only prove himself but also improve himself and come forth accomplished in the end. Because the prince accepts the commands and conditions of the confrontation, he prepares himself correctly for the challenges of his future task and puts in order what is necessary for it.

The "inner fire" is always drawn to certain tests or trials before receiving a higher or more rarefied existence. By undertaking such trials, one subjects oneself to the test of reality. Indeed, viewed from the other side, one can perceive how reality becomes more favourable when it is shown that the right commitment is present and one is successful via the ordeals that are prepared through such commitment. Once it has been proven that one has a right to be there and to take one's worthy place, one comes to obtain the *middle* power of fire—that is to say, the inner direction with which decisions can be addressed.

The unknown area here concerns the question of how best to struggle through the challenges that life now offers. At this juncture, one develops the strength and vision to face the challenges of life by creating one's own assignments even though it may happen that in a given enterprise, one assigns the carrying out of certain tasks to others. In either case, the purpose is essentially the same: to minimise oppositions so that they become negotiable. The King is the designer of these commands.

(3)

Wands ◊

THE KNIGHT

3rd step:
Directing
the assignments

It is the Knight who is the most skilful in solving tasks because he is the executor of them and serves the ideas that were designed in advance. The emphasis in this phase lies in a different kind of unknown territory. It is not the Knight's task to invent assignments that will minimise confrontations. The most important element for him is the development of a technique that permits him to perform tasks well. The Knight has to work the longest to mature and to prepare himself for the task. Moreover, he has to spend the most time on it and knows that by slowly learning to extend a technique, he is forthwith more capable of converting challenges to his advantage, and subsequently his chances of success will be increased. His inner fire may be thought of as a form of "tactics" combined with an overview of the situation. As a result of this skill, he becomes mature enough to handle large or small enterprises—even those that have nothing to do with him—and to defend a certain vision that he stands behind. Here, much more has been competently handled when compared with the Prince, who has still to conquer his place as King. The Knight is also able to cope with aims other than his own because the cause of an aim does not need to lie within him. Each command for which he has the strength he will avidly support providing that it tallies with his basic vision. At the prompting of a certain command, he will attempt to give direction to his personal assignment. However, the unknown area here never relates to the description of these assignments. The Knight takes care that the talent will possess the fortitude to handle multiple tasks.

(4)

Wands

THE PAGE

4th step: Enthusiasm

When the nature of one's tasks is known and one can estimate both the causes and the consequences of them, all this then becomes confidential, and one can fully commit oneself to them remaining somewhere in the middle, in a state of balance. This stage is called the Page. Here, when the undertaking automatically provides the feed, one can muster enthusiasm for it and simply let the energy flow. This is a stance where the entire flow can be easily implemented and where the consequences are secondary to the direct flow itself.

(5)

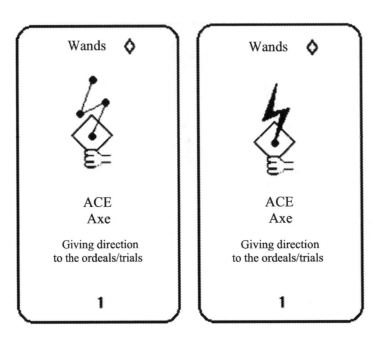

When one takes the initiative, participating fully in all the naturally occurring consequences arising from assuming such responsibility, one takes into account the overall flow of energy involved in it and the nature of its ordeals. One even begins to decide for oneself when such trials occur. This attitude of active independence in the midst of confrontations is called Axis or Ace.

From the perspective of the outside world, it is no longer certain where trials begin or where consequences are produced. Here, one alters the moment at will and even suggests and approves one's most appropriate points for initiating and ceasing. For instance, expressing a target as a condition is one possible perspective that, having already defined itself, leads to new results and causes. And since the energy confronting one is sufficient to cause such a confrontational area, one can easily launch a series of trials able to direct the life cycle's purposes without, however, knowing with any certainty where these will emerge from.

(6)

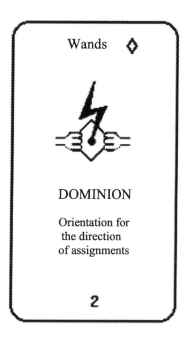

The articulation of one's own "objectives" causes reactions that, in the course of time, develop their own methods of how to handle these objectives. In fact, we know very well that when selecting certain formulations, the rules of the game change alongside them. By applying this intelligence, one understands the initial cause and can therefore predict a degree of its impact. Here, one has the responsibility to determine not what but *how* something is put in place. Therefore, one pays special attention as to how best face these trials or confrontations. One pays careful attention to discover the most appropriate moment to express them. This stance we call Dominion: learning to watch patiently over a whole realm of possibilities to discover where confrontations with one's intentions can have the most favourable consequences. This involves a particular kind of prescience capable of discerning the likely success of matters before launching forth into something new. Here, one pays attention not only to the environment or the chosen working area but also, horizontally, to how confrontations or trials can unfold further and find new fields of application.

One will not only deal with the outer implications but also deal similarly and simultaneously with one's own inner foundations. Where both kinds of working area are able to work towards one cooperative energy stream—in the horizontal sense of application as well as in the vertical sense of stimulation—then there is scope in between for success because both working areas coincide in making an effort towards it.

(7)

Wands ◇

MAKING
A
VIRTUE
OF NEED

3

When one becomes familiar with all the possibilities existing within a momentarily triggered confrontation field, one notes the presence of certain needs requiring attention to establish a more continuous equilibrium. To allow for a further balancing out, plans should be improved and sufficiently prepared for in such a way that during the confrontation process, these may be improved further.

When later it may appear that there were crudities in the planning, one would then not lose face. For while this may provide a good opportunity to identify weaknesses, it also offers a chance to discover and distil strengths or at least to identify an opportunity to make adjustments so that any weaknesses may still be converted into strengths. To confront this kind of situation can become a "strong point." The needs in question then need not be destructive but can be converted into virtues.

The research conducted here may even deliberately look at these needs to consciously determine what might possibly cause eventual confrontations. On the other hand, if one refuses to look at and deal with the central aspect of this card—making a virtue into a need—it will cause problems. However, by remaining connected with this continuous investigation into causes, one maintains a watch over the smooth operation of the whole.

(8)

Wands ◊

REPLENISHMENT

Uniting
activities

Each wand is the symbolic representation of a staff, which acts as a support for a leading figure or position of power. In English, the word "staff" suggests such positions of power as in the case of the employees in a workplace. The plural of the Dutch word for "staff" is *staven* and is the Dutch word used for this series. Staven, in its active form as a verb, relates to the idea of testing. Thus, we have meanings of the word staven such as to endorse or to check if and how things are working.

As mentioned previously, the S rune-like energy of the wand expresses its energy by focusing and directing it. In this direction and focus, we can recognise three parts. The *lower part* or base of the "fire ordeal" stands for the challenges one encounters in life. The *middle part* undergoes or endures these challenges and may be considered as the point of friction through which one senses the differences and combinations. It is the part that takes care of linking the most active compounds. The last or *upper part* refers to the impact and the consequences of all these confrontations.[7]

We can only sense this fire energy from one angle at a time. Either we see it from the point of view of the confronter, ambitiously seeking to change reality, or we see it from the perspective of the receiver, the one confronted with a reality that may appear very different from how he or she previously perceived it. This stage, which we have designated here as "Replenishment," confronts the effects of a person's ambition to change or not to change, and seeks to do something with this idea. In this phase, one is dealing with the fact that confrontations can happen from two sides or from two points of view.

One can expect that certain contradictions emerging from the area of confrontation will be emphasised and come together with increasing effect. Only in a more complete region of confrontation based on a realistic balance between the opposites can the contradictions merge and intersect and thereby bring together into the same working area both the cause of the one who cannot see the effects as well the effects of the one who cannot not see the cause. This new joint working area thus becomes something

---

[7] The Reader may find it helpful to consider here the cardinal, fxed, and mutable modes of fire as well as the three traditional centres of the human organism: navel – like the "guts" (instinctive—cardinal), heart (emotional—fixed)/, head (mental—mutable).

quite different: a more viable place simultaneously taking account of original causes and ultimate effects. For he who understands this area, the tension here is considered a welcome challenge preceding any achievement.

(9)

It becomes clear at this juncture that everyone seeks to achieve something personal. One can do a lot more than just try to maintain a balance between ambitions. One has to realise that one may indeed have a will of one's own and also a desire to fit this will into existence without "damaging" the whole. This kind of endeavour leads to an understanding, which results in a classification of tasks within the greater whole. One comes to understand that several trial areas may occur simultaneously, each with their own challenges while all still managing to fit within the whole.

Not everyone or every task or every opinion need be confronted, but the responsibilities of each will receive attention in certain partial areas. One learns that a breakdown of tasks can allow differing opinions to live alongside each other just as long as they all continue to assist the development of the whole. Personal ideals cannot always find a place of accord yet may still cause the best result within their appointed work area. For each individual, this sort of "striving" to do is a necessity, which works to expand personal responsibilities. To attain this goal, it will be necessary to keep an eye on additional tasks or challenges within these work areas.

(10)

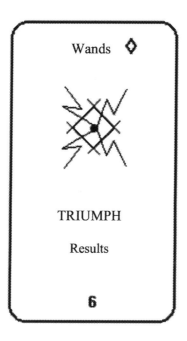

Wands ◊

TRIUMPH

Results

6

The one who is able to increase his or her responsibility over many areas at once and allow each area to have its different effect will receive the sum of many results, which, in turn, will serve to strengthen the whole. The card that expresses this idea is called Victory or Triumph.

One has become "master" over a variety of activities and now receives the crowning glory for all the work one has put into these activities. This victory is not earned through the possession of abilities alone but, more especially, by *results*. The more results delivered, the more victorious the feeling. This feeling of victory will be less in the case of a political jostle to acquire a given function than it will for the one who manages to work his or her way up from the bottom. In the latter case, one knows there are already many results brewing. At this point, the feeling of victory itself can be somewhat sweltering. Hence, caution is appropriate here because this card is associated with another testing ground. Simply being satisfied with one's performances is not sufficiently binding. A 'wreath' is actually woven into the present pattern bound between results. It is only here that the energy remains potent enough to earn lasting good (in terms of causes and effects). Further victory depends on the extent of the contacts one has acquired through one's activities. In this sense, one *is* one's activity, and with this mentality, each activity will be continued.

(11)

Wands ◊

BRAVERY

Further possibilities
with risk

7

In any enterprise, it is not perceived as obvious and perhaps not even recommended that one keep an eye on every component with the same degree of focus. It might happen that a particular component needs more attention or—if it has already received additional attention—there is also no guarantee that it will work out by maintaining this kind of focus. There is always the risk of losing control over the basic energy because some branches no longer seem to belong to the original root. To have them comply to a single power, and work as an extension of one source, "Bravery" or "Courage" is necessary. Bravery and courage are needed to confront and deal with this and also to rearrange one's own intention to obtain something from the source for further improvement.

This means that every unfamiliar challenge demands extra attention. It is always a challenge to make things fit within one central movement. There is always the danger another interest will prevail or become dominant. This might be experienced as a threat, but it can also be experienced as a challenge, which keeps the dynamism of the whole powerful without compromising the integrity of "independent parts." One may still permit small deviations so long as these do not interfere with the functioning of the main power.

(12)

One might try to keep everything under control, but just then it may happen that one hasty decision causes all the energy to be transmitted in a direction that does not lead to a balanced result. One comes to the conclusion that some decisions have been made rather hastily and did not receive thorough preparation. Of course, this refers to a situation in which a number of unknown factors has played a role and one felt the pressure of expectation that certain quick decisions were required from someone. Now a new sort of confrontational area has arisen as a result of too many hasty decisions. One begins to notice the kind of things one has overlooked and where one could have exercised a more circumspect response. One also notices what has been neglected at the expense of these quick decisions and transactions. By attending to the possibility that this may happen again, one begins to reflect on this and to reconsider the importance of correct timing. The issue here is not about whether to reverse a decision made but about the presence of a new confrontation area involving a compromise in which one begins to recognise what has come about as a result of imperfect timing and insufficient consideration of the information necessary to form the appropriate judgements to make decisions.

Allowing this new confrontation area to work towards a clarification of one's shortcomings, one manages to turn this situation into one in which such weaknesses are confronted. When one knows this confrontation area is present, one gives it extra attention so that the possibility of premature decisions is pre-cognised and arrested. This said it is, of course, still possible that even in hastiness, one has managed to make the right decisions. Wrong verdicts could also be validated in which attention was too quickly divided within the whole. This nature of this kind of division is a general consequence for everyone who shares in this field of confrontation.

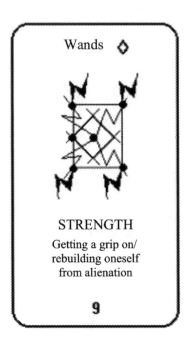

In all of this, there is no cause for worry since even in cases of wrong decisions, one is able to quickly return to them and insert a new structure into them. This is about being strong in a situation where one is pressed into acknowledging facts that have already emerged on a few occasions or which have repeatedly changed their nature or where certain difficulties have occurred and one has had to react to them. This new field of confrontation restores the original power of "action and reaction." How one tackles confrontations in general is coming up for inspection now. A lot of confrontations arising from opinions or from driving forces requiring the restoration of primordial energy will make a path through one, and it is primarily how one faces up to these forces that will determine whether there is balance. Not to defend opinions is essential here. He who is convinced that such activity is based on a sound principle is able to become stronger from hereon.

(14)

The last and final card in this series is called Oppression, which expresses the direct consequence of an excessive re-coordination for the purposes of control. In fact, this control has always been the intention in this area, which is so heavily focused on confrontation. Discipline and obedience are considered acquired talents of the dominant whole. But enforced discipline can never keep either a business or an activity running. Somehow, one must retain the feeling that one still has a viable place to go to. To reach a "free space," it is necessary to have a certain degree of coordinating strength that can function independently. Ultimately, anything that is necessary for one is lost by breaking certain bonds of control over them. The confrontation area here is valid for oneself as well as for others. To discover how the action-reaction transactions can still be achieved is the unknown factor here, the completely free terrain in which one can formulate thoughts, feelings, results, and attitudes. The "liveable place" is now more important than what one wishes to accomplish within it.

The statement "quid pro quo" is added beneath the above card because one must know that if one chooses to commit to this or that choice, what will come forth from this choice will be a corresponding fit. This means that something else cannot come forth from it. Hence, it is that coordination is always accompanied by a form of *oppression*. Of course, this is no bad thing as long as one pays attention to it and recognises the fact that one "places" the justified and excludes the unjust or the incorrect. What can help develop our insight further into this acquired freedom will constitute the next suit or series of cards.

4

SPADES/SWORDS/
TRIALS BY AIR

Learning to assess restrictions: dealing with thoughts

It is helpful to pay attention to environments to see whether one can inhabit them and whether they will remain habitable with the help of the *mental faculties*, represented here by the suit of Spades or Swords. The necessary liberties can only be attained by means of the powers of *discernment* and *differentiation* characteristic of the Sword.

(1)

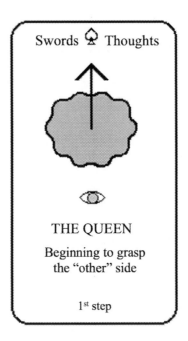

The first card of this series is once more the Queen. Her vision begins by observing things from a distance as if they were taking place outside of her own life. In this phase, one removes oneself from all that lies outside one's ordinary field of perception, outside one's personal confrontation field, and outside one's immediate working environment. This particular stance of "keeping one's distance" and remaining "outside" is a first condition and a necessary attitude to develop before possessing the ability to *make distinctions with the sword*. However, one must realise that with this attitude, one will no longer be a part of the dependent rhythms driving the life course. This attitude bestows the benefit of being able to place everything that appears foreign to oneself into a comprehensible learning opportunity without actually having to be part of it. In this way, one can gain insight into things that have nothing to do with one's own life or life course.

Wherever the emotion or confrontation is most directly connected, the mind is hereby able to maintain the necessary distance to sustain an independent view.

(2)

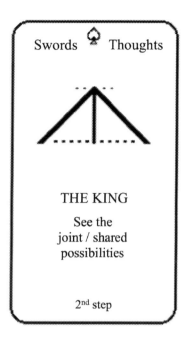

The King of Swords gains a sufficient grasp of the facts as to undertake something with them. The purpose here is to achieve more clarity with respect to matters. "Insight" arises from a certain source, which brings with it discernment through the powers of *differentiation* and *separation*. Yet it also brings together elements through *synthesis*. This whole process entails the talent of using one's rational mind. Sharpening this sword of reason means learning to perceive and discover potential possibilities.

One finds there are always ways in which one is able to think clearer or apply one's reasoning more effectively. Everyone has a personal talent wherein the rational mind's capacity for vision and distinction is operating best. The emphasis here is not on the expression, acquisition, or realisation of intellectual faculties but on the willingness to find a place for them. *Consideration* is one of the secondary factors present in the rational faculties.

(3)

The Knight of Swords shows *alertness* and, in this way, makes use of all the realisations achieved. He nourishes his mind with everything that can teach him *persuasiveness*. With this gift, he is able to succeed in his activities. The Knight is the best executive of any well-thought-out plan. By understanding the plan, the source of inspiration from whence it came becomes much larger. Through the inspiration of the Knight, one receives more power, which can then be included in the implementation and direction of any given plan.

For the Knight, formulated objectives evolve naturally into a synthesis, which ultimately brings a unity of thought as well as a certain vigour and determination. In this phase, the thinking of each aspirant will automatically achieve a certain radicalisation. It is only possible to be really propelled forward by this "radical thinking" when the seedbed for it is sufficiently substantial. When this proves to be the case, the future prospects are equally extensive.

The unknown territory in this stage concerns the potential outcome of such incorporation. Fortunately, the fundamental will shall be fed from a source of insight and so can shape itself and adapt itself through this sort of seedbed. This makes the mental activity *enterprising*.

(4)

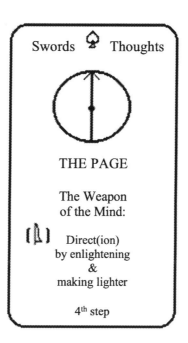

Swords ♠ Thoughts

THE PAGE

The Weapon
of the Mind:

Direct(ion)
by enlightening
&
making lighter

4th step

While the weapon of the mind is strengthened by method, it also needs a direction to go in. The rational mind seeks to translate things into methods and theories, but this functions best when the rational faculty can make the work in question more practical. Laws and theories were first invented to make life easier for us so that the following of the law would always remain available to us. This is the area where one can test theories and laws and check if they are still appropriate or whether something needs to be changed.

The "feather of truth"—as seen balanced against the heart on the pans of the Great Scale in the Scene of the Weighing of the Soul from the Temple of Der-el-Medinet—possesses the lightness of a feather. This "lightness" means that the whole of the truth with which we are dealing here cannot be "heavy," burdensome, or difficult for us. To face truth honestly is to undo what is heavy by wielding our sword. The arrow in the Page of Swords is like the hand of a clock ready to steer in any direction. It is important when we undertake the process of "reasoning" that we are able to articulate truth in its absolute simplicity. In this way, our life can be released from any objections and freed from weight. The Page is a symbol of a servant who senses what is best for the future.

(5)

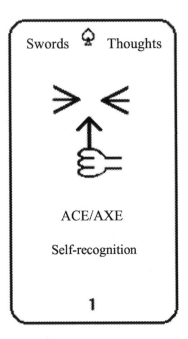

Now that one grasps how one's rational processes work best and how one is fit to undertake a given task by articulating oneself clearly, the moment arrives in which one is able to "handle" one's *ratio* and use it as a tool. In respect of ideas, one is not biased towards principles or objectives that conform to the outside world. The mind has now gained the ability to distinguish unpleasant things and to take care of matters. While the environment of Hearts or Cups easily distinguishes what is most pleasant (or agreeable) or most productive of incorporation, the mental distinction afforded by the suit of Swords need not be experienced as discomfort or unpleasantness. The outer form of rational thought is only for those who are anxious to avoid its distinctions.

The Axis or Ace of Swords is no sensitive wench. The Dutch word for "wench," *wicht*, reminds one of *gewicht,* or "weight," suggesting a "weighty" person who shows pressure in a situation. The Ace is a ruthless figure who seeks to gain control over situations—to determine chalk lines/to go and pull the strings. So be warned! However, this is nothing to be afraid of. Nor will it hurt. Even he who governs is a pauper.

A proper wielding of the sword is only possible with the apposite self-criticism. A sword does not bring the critical aspect alone and only works well when one has learned to relativise its use. With the appearance of the situation that this card represents, the moment has come for such relative utilisation. In essence, the aim of the sword is to bring clarity. One still wants to perceive opportunities, be able to defy dangers, and also be one's own protector and helper. The unknown here is simply what one will inevitably encounter. Let it come.

(6)

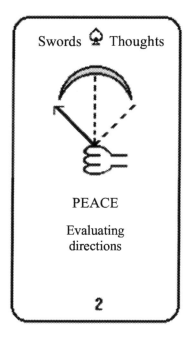

Swords ♠ Thoughts

PEACE

Evaluating
directions

2

To proceed, the sword does not have to pave a way by force. As the above card suggests, the proper application of the sword is Peace. How does thought follow a peaceful course? How can it produce anything without having to fight for it? The answer is by learning to evaluate things by means of careful comparison and deliberation, weighing up situations in a state of ease. Any interference by the pressures of emotion or instinctual urges will cause one to no longer be open to a correct assessment of the situation. The activation of the rational capacity is precisely intended to counter such dependencies. The rational mind ought to judge without *pre*judgement and to acknowledge facts as facts. In this way, then, the facts themselves can be channelled in a direction without one feeling enslaved by them. Of course, surrounding circumstances and emotions and such like are also facts, but they are now no longer determining factors in whether something should or should not be done.

The ancient idea of preventing the advance of demons with the aid of a cross originally stems from the image of two intersecting swords held up before the demons as a gesture proclaiming, "Cease ye the struggle of dependence!" Think rationally, then, and no longer look at what displeases or discourages you or at what you like or dislike or have doubts about because all of this simply blinds you in the moment. It is much more important to find out where the mind is able to find peace because in the "place of peace," the mind is most capable of reasoning. When being subject to some form of discontent—in Dutch, this word is called *onvrede*, equivalent to a state of un-peace—one loses one's rational ability and some of one's vital energy to that dissatisfaction. If, however, one can articulate precisely how one is ready for something, one is then taking action to regain one's rational abilities.

(7)

Because of emotional confrontations when we describe certain contradictions in the heart as facts, this provokes a fightback from a third-edged sword in such a way that the reality of these contradictions becomes an insurmountable fact that one will also have to deal with. But one does not know how to deal with this new conflict because, thus far, one has only had the talent of description. It is the apparently insurmountable obstruction proposed by this new situation that makes it appear like "Doom." Moreover, not only is the inevitable fact of these contradictions feels so serious and gloomy but also an aspect of this conflicted energy now crosses beyond the faculty of thought begging to lose its efficacy. Facts have been driven in an undesirable direction, and now the mind cannot come up with anything else other than what would make it worse by pushing it further in the same direction. However, there is also a positive side to this process that is able to cast a light on everything that is "stuck."

The positive side of this process leads to the understanding that the entire enclosed unit will be opened up because the rational mind *itself* is like a "locked-up force" from whence its condition of reasoning comes. It is the "self" that, in this "rational" way, will be lost and set against the correspondences of the heart (which is now able to "feel" life more directly). When the mind operated alone, it appeared to block or obstruct itself by perceiving all its contradictions. In point of fact, it was the disengaging or untwisting of this energy that had been the source of its *raison d'être*.

Hence, the unknown territory in this phase is all those results coming from this kind of rational "loss." It could be forced further in a different direction by adopting a more compassionate mode of thinking that takes into account many more facts than its own rationalisation process. Perhaps this process hasn't been so reasonable after all! One is now forced to take into account a larger section of reality than what one has previously been accustomed to reason about. One must learn to become more "reasonable" through the capacity to see what is causing the darkness in one's own reasoning processes.

We repeat then that the power of the Sword is meant to lighten. Dark and heavy thoughts merely indicate restrictions and stand for the limitations of the Sword. One is only able to turn the intelligence of the Sword to its proper task when one surpasses the merely utilitarian methods of reasoning one is already familiar with.

(8)

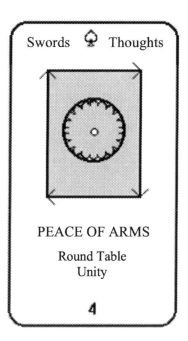

Here, one is able to take into account the fact that mental faculties do not originate from learned and established ideas but are a generally applicable power that can work in any place where rational construction is required. So, at this point, simply relying on one's own abilities and insights is no longer taken too seriously. One now knows that the reasoning process can be effectively put into operation just about anywhere. One knows that one can formulate something in a reasonable way and need not focus too much on the successful results of such reasoning. In addition, it is no longer essential that one prove oneself through thinking or that one comes across in a convincing way, able to propagate this or that conviction. From the moment one succeeds in leaving behind the arrogant belief in the rational method, one can reasonably leave reason to its own devices.

The swords are thus arranged in such a way that they do not necessarily have to do something. The conditioning of the mind is set because the nature of the mind includes its own mindset (even without action). It needs nothing more than trust, faith, and a constancy towards Wisdom. There is no need to preach because that faith itself has the essential purpose of maintaining a balance from within. The true elements that remain attached to this belief are only strong when the effect of a natural morality and balance become firmly connected to one other. This card is sometimes called "Armour," but here we prefer to give it the title "Unity of the Round Table." This is because the Knights of the Round Table used to lay down their weapons on this table before they proceeded to discuss anything. The purpose of this gesture was to encourage unity of thought.

Here, no desire for domination continues to plays a role in affairs. Instead, the gesture of laying down one's weapons brings the power of the whole back into a management zone wherein each individual's actions stay in balance.

Throughout history, round tables have existed based on this original precursor. Yet this concept of the "round table" can only work effectively with a mediator who can ensure the condition that one put one's sword on the table during an argument with the express aim of achieving a common goal.

(9)

Of course, it may happen that in the presence of a weak link, there may occur certain difficulties. During a joint cooperation, this weak link will reveal a flaw—creating an imminent sense that the swords will no longer remain upon the table with their points directed to the centre but will be picked up for a fight in a confined place. Since unity was the objective from the start, this force has been tied together by a certain "strength," which will acknowledge and place this weaker spot. At the point of trouble, its duty is to put this weakness in its right place—namely, at the place of "defeat." In recognising weaknesses, the acceptance of its lesser place produces healing.

The sword does not necessarily need to engage in a struggle here. By facing confrontation, the sword is meant to replace such weaknesses and reveal that the mental function is able to offer a more practical point of view. When it is unclear where, or at which point, the weak place is to be found, the Court of Justice may offer help. The weak (victim) or the weak link (abuse of power) can still use this opportunity to offer all general weaknesses an open and critical focus. In any case, only an authority representative of the most common power can bring the necessary solace to redirect one towards the duty of humility and respect in relation to the general activity.

In general, one can say that what is revealed here is a situation that "oppresses" one because of one's present weaknesses. To overcome this situation, one can do nothing else but place this form of pressure (and weight) and with it suppress the weaknesses. This presupposes a certain repression that is necessary here to ensure balance. It is important to know the *weaknesses of the arguments* and to put better arguments before acknowledged strengths. Of minor importance is the testing of familiar interrogation methods because these are likely to bring contradictions into the practical implementation of the known totality. For now, what is most important is the stress laid upon the "subordinate place" of the weaknesses and the arguments used to support them.

(10)

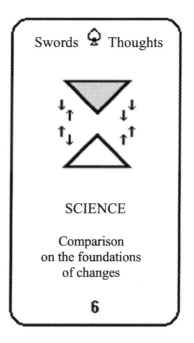

Swords ♤ Thoughts

SCIENCE

Comparison
on the foundations
of changes

6

Without a method to distinguish the "weaknesses" from what is "strong" makes discernment very difficult and dependent on the vigour of the arguments advanced. It is the task of "science" to develop a method that will lead more easily to what needs to be changed in a given direction. This method assists one in moving more easily through difficulties. It has a working ground, which, thanks to some tactics, leads swiftly to results or to a situation where the student of such science can progress further than would be the case if working without such a method. For this reason, a scientist is not the same as someone who simply experiences the facts but, thanks to his developed techniques, is someone who can use method or "tricks of thought" to generate insights and understanding.

(11)

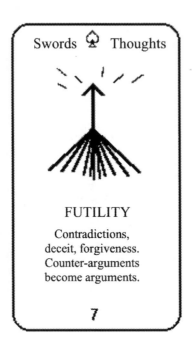

Swords ♠ Thoughts

FUTILITY

Contradictions,
deceit, forgiveness.
Counter-arguments
become arguments.

7

"Absolution" is one of the instructive directions provided by this card. So many contradictions come together here that any penalising action against the presenting facts when dealing with these kinds of reactions will not leave anything constructive to maintain a society. Within a large number of contradictions, removing the so-called bad sides would only turn each problem into something completely fruitless in advance. To review a situation, a complete recast is necessary so as not to leave anything as it is or was before.

Forgiveness will show up here as a concept because there is still much good to draw from the situation. "Forgiving" here means learning to understand the origins and motives of an altered and destabilised situation. Intrigues often have something cunning about them because they use back doors to achieve their goals. Yet it sometimes happens that the intrigue itself is inspired by a fear of not achieving the goal through the detour that is made.

Focusing too much on what went wrong and on what was ill-conceived only makes everything more complicated, less practical, and increasingly unpleasant. Of course, this does not mean that the original goals existing in society will become more easily accessible simply by knowing the conditions of how to get there. Humans will still look for easy ways to provide them with a goal even if the goal is still premature and they themselves still immature. It is more conducive to describe the steps by means of which one may meet the conditions to shape those steps into something concrete with opportunities for growth, improvement, and adaptation towards the goal. It is a task of the rational mind to acquire the sufficient responsibility that will permit society to achieve its goals more easily through direct targets. It is, of course, true that the existence of an easy detour with many disadvantages is as much a disease for the whole of society as it is for those who use these as interim solutions. Only by fully recognising the original goals themselves can one work towards fashioning certain goals with purified arguments.

It is valuable to contemplate this whole process of transformation here described and learn to deal with the prime "possibilities of goals" through a range of potentials rather than opting for the easy routes already existing that have been shown to oppress and suppress everything. The middle sword in the drawing of this card indicates the desire for the "middle road." The talent treated of here is used to convert an unproductive situation into suitable conditions for new proposals.

(12)

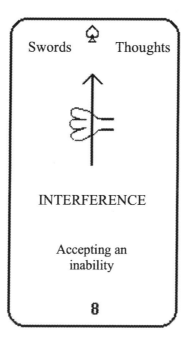

When there exist more counterarguments than arguments, one may fall upon one's sword. This is the moment of withdrawal or retreat. This is the moment where one needs to accept one's own inability (powerlessness or impotence). The way to do this is not by grasping at the situation in an attempt to get a better grip on it because now the situation is like a sharp sword. To let go and surrender with acceptance allows the self-created blindfold and cuffs to fall off and the hopelessness of the situation to which one feels bound to slowly subside. Here, one is in abeyance to a "force majeure." Only being quiet and knowing how and when to quit will help the situation. Not every "theory" fits in practice, and, in this case, the practice is not open to your theory. The best attitude to adopt here is silence.

(13)

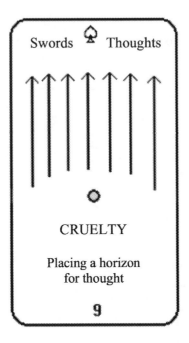

Swords ♠ Thoughts

CRUELTY

Placing a horizon
for thought

9

The next card is called "Cruelty" because it is a cruel experience to realise that everything one has previously thought about things has to be verified in terms of how things actually are in practice. This more practical aspect is an even harsher reality than accepting the arguments of good intentions. No good intention by itself causes something good and fitting to happen. On the other hand, one can also say that no derogation or deflection necessarily leads to bad consequences either. In fact, experiencing one's own thoughts is not synonymous with a force that keeps everything under control. The horizon on which one's own thoughts are placed might constitute a reality, but this does not necessarily make it a place one would want to go to. The other side of this condition is that one also learns that every kind of thinking is permitted and may have a right to expression within a context that exists beforehand and that cannot be predicted. The cruelty of existence also brings the recognition of one's own—as well as others—unique individuality, the realisation that each individual has the right to exist and to take its own shape or structure. Even though apparently there may exist a plethora of differently formed opinions, one's own articulation will gain an actuality in a larger context and will receive a particular place in it that cannot be predicted.

It seems at first sight as though the horizon of perspectives being offered here distributes all possibilities in a random manner. The fact that the determinacy of the changing decisions has no predictability at all, it is already in evidence. The individuality is still appreciated, but the self-will of how and where to perform or achieve something is secondary and should be subordinate because the freedom of society cannot be forced to surrender. It is only at the moment when this individuality is tested in the practice of a larger context that it can really create something good there. This means that the sooner you recognise the places where you can go, the better. If one prefers to force conditions for the expression of one's own abilities, one remains on a hopelessly forced quest. When the mind puts extra energy into learning where (at each moment) something fits, it begins to accept larger and more fertile perspectives, which, in turn, put into perspective the limitations of idealism without losing any of its individual faculties.

Thus, this atmosphere only appears cruel because one discovers how different individuals have the ability to see things in distinctly different ways. Looking for the "appropriate place" becomes the unknown territory here.

(14)

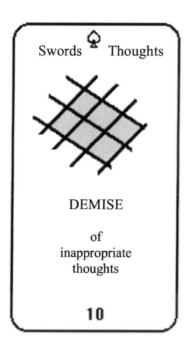

In reality, we learn that there are some thoughts that do not work and others that, on the contrary, impart strength. Renouncing unsuitable thoughts sets the mind free to explore. The last card in the suit of Swords is entitled "Demise" (or "Collapse"). Unproductive ideas render defective that with which one was mentally involved and cause a rupture with any method one was working with. The mental possibilities are really all outside oneself, in fact, fully in the *unknown*. Anyone who continues experiencing what is known or familiar begins to suffer from its demise. One can also grow out of such presuppositions when one realises that they are for the most part primitive, restrictive, and deal with the perception of reduced contexts. The unknown territory here is anything "thinkable" that we do not yet know. All the rest is dark and obscure. Perhaps it is simply not imaginable (in a rational way). Perhaps it is itself the result of everything, which is the only essence remaining here.

How one may create and learn to deal with practical results will be explored further in the next series. For now, learning to see practical results (directly) is the new and unknown area here.

5

CLUBS/PENTACLES/COINS/
TRIALS BY EARTH

Learning the nature of exchange: dealing with coins or "pure results"

(1)

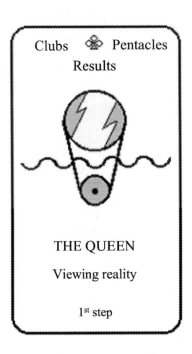

The Queen of Pentacles (Stars/Coins/Results) is the first card of this series. "Coins" are a useful symbol to represent results because the energy we put to use in our daily lives is primarily materialised and exchanged as money. Recall here the biblical currency of *talents*. "Stars," on the other hand, suggest a more idealistic context compared with that of "coins." Thus, the Pentagram or Star is a symbol for a result that is part of a much larger context and as a follow-up to certain achievements. The circular form of the Pentacle represents a more circumscribed and bound result, which is the reason that this suit is also sometimes called "Disks."

Whoever has managed to implement or at least become familiar with the previous series of cards and their various attitudes knows that reality—as orientation and outcome—need not be a "positive achievement." If results are achieved, those results become "neutral," even when they have been realised from a number of different arguments. A "result" has nothing to do with a mental assumption. Nor is it an ideal representation formed in the heart, some sort of functional working area in which one can defend oneself against other realities or through which one can find one's own sort of reality and discover things to be more of a reality by being activated by "confrontations." A "result" in this vein has only value to the extent that it has a practical right to exist within a certain period of a particular individual's existence. To get to know the *sum total of results* means *focusing on the useful*, regardless of how this usefulness is understood.

In this card or phase, one initially considers the sum of one's own value(s) represented here by the small circle in the drawing and reflects this through a certain practical curriculum (which exists in a more common context).

(2)

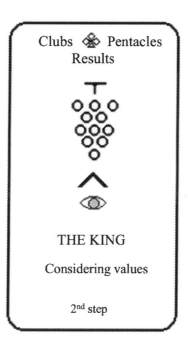

Only after a lot of work do the fruits of endeavour come to a certain maturity or condition of ripeness. Only after a certain period of maturity do things attain the right to exist and can be truly considered as constituting a "result." Only after passing through a certain period of development can one make it to that maturity. Fruits that mature quickly always "taste" a little light and may prove acceptable in a temporary context. On the other hand, fruits that come to maturity only after difficult labour and much struggle are for the connoisseur.

The King of Coins takes care in particular that his *presentation* looks good because his judgement will depend upon it. As to what in the end the result will be used for, this will be determined by a different kind of cognition. The first foundation for its appearance is the finished condition of the product. Only then can it be considered a finished product and a real result with a degree of maturity. Here, one will have to decide for oneself what kind of qualities are able to be worked out within the results. What can be simultaneously integrated here are the "values" behind results, their context, and their importance.

(3)

It is mainly the Knight who will propagate certain *values*. For the Knight, these values bring him dignity, which he then conveys to others. His task is difficult. The "maturity of results" is what is most important to him along with the unfolding of his personality, his honour, his chivalry, and his ability to honestly express himself. The search for places where this can become a practical reality for him is his area of exploration.

(4)

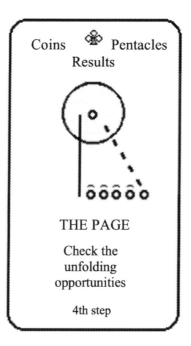

The Page of pentacles is very dependent on his or her talents. At the same time, he or she can also draw the best out of them and unfold them truly as his or her own. Here, the task is how to distinguish which ideals yield something fruitful and which among them allow for the possibility for something to happen. The unfolding of opportunities proceeds here almost automatically.

(5)

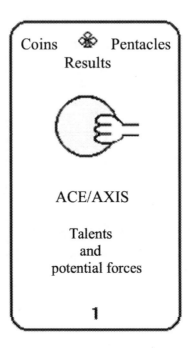

When the fruits one has within one's grasp are relevant to the life path, they are then ripe and ready to be carried out and manifested. One has, at the same time, a sense of certain opportunities wherein one can organise these results, which come forth as achievements from the previous cards or stages. By knowing this, one can "handle" results well and can count on one's "talent" or potential as a solid basis for results. This is the "Axis" or "Ace" of Pentacles. Its whole nature is revealing itself. It is deeply connected with the dynamics of life itself. Hence, the image of the "Star" (or Pentacle) as a sign for this suit, which links it with astrology and an aspect of destiny that we are able to control or at least take into our own hands. Thus, "Coins" and "Talents" can certainly be *exchanged* the one for the other. Of course, coins and talents are not entirely synonymous. But when things are well founded, both may appear simultaneously with results. The talent that is commonly ascribed to Coins indicates the likelihood of its alignment with reality. Just how, where, and by what means this talent is going to so align is the unknown territory here.

(6)

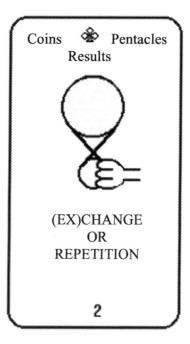

Coins   Pentacles
Results

(EX)CHANGE
OR
REPETITION

2

One can now say that one is applying one's talents in something like a profession. The talent can develop when the type of work is varied and interesting or it can flat line in a mundane and repetitive grind. The extent to which one is able to play with things and keep them interesting is dependent on the "form" in which one's talents are being shaped. Here, the unknown is to discover how best to continue to develop in the context of one's work.

(7)

Here, one is tied to a certain "constancy" that may or may not have fashioned a form of fortitude in one's personal life. The question that emerges here is whether one is looking only to the usefulness of this "work" or whether one is concerned about its capacity to support the superior values in one's life. Outside of one's given talents or one's profession, it requires an extra effort to make everything fit and work together. In other words, one must maintain the *original intention*. If one succeeds in this, then the results can bring great satisfaction and, of course, genuine support.

(8)

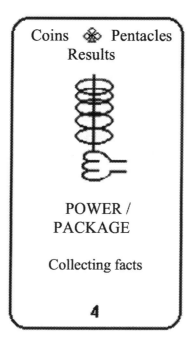

Coins ❖ Pentacles
Results

POWER /
PACKAGE

Collecting facts

4

When work gives satisfaction, one can surround oneself with the results and exude a proportionate degree of personal power. To assist in this, one surrounds oneself with all that one has achieved. The sense of "having accomplished something" can be felt by someone who is rich in some manner and is able to benefit from this power. This assembling of assets about the individual need not be paraded or personally profited from, since it has a "power of presentation" projected as it were from a larger whole.

The unknown territory here is how *others* handle this expression of power and whether they feel they are becoming limited by it or that their freedom of communication is being compromised by it. If the presentation itself is balanced and the individual's personal wealth permits them to act completely and integrally, then direct communication is no longer a problem. Clarifying in this respect will be the surrounding cards or the general context in which "power" is presented. Thus far, this card possesses only potential power. The effects it will cause at inappropriate moments remains unknown terrain.

(9)

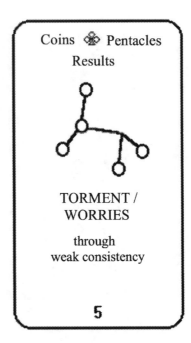

When spontaneous communication becomes limited in others, the new circumscribed unity of facts within this context can become a torment and a burden. One begins to worry about the possible inconsistency of future communications or about the contrasts the aforementioned elements built up now entail. Awareness begins to emerge that for others it may be a burden to be cast into the shadow of this "wealth." In fact, it is only what is truly "necessary" and linked to the "useful" that will survive any further evolution. This card acknowledges the weak correlation between parts that become estranged from one another because of the imbalance that gathered too many talents somewhere and too little elsewhere.

(10)

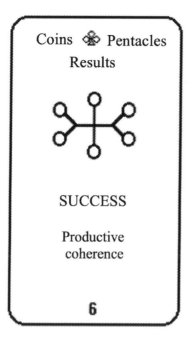

Coins ❖ Pentacles
Results

SUCCESS

Productive
coherence

6

The success of this constant accretion is thus dependent on the balance that has been accomplished by oneself *combined with* the result this causes on others. A productive relationship between results is noticeable in situations where public opinion and needs can be measured. There must exist someplace a relationship between the needs of the environment and the achievements of the individual.

(11)

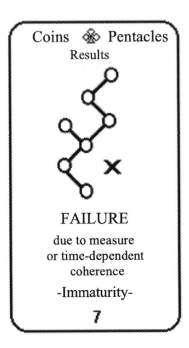

Coins ✦ Pentacles

Results

FAILURE

due to measure
or time-dependent
coherence

-Immaturity-

7

Sometimes, it happens that there cannot be found at the same time a talent (or talents) and a public ready to appreciate them. In any case, talents should be matured over a significant period before they are made presentable. The integration process is also time dependent and is a private working area that has to be laboured upon before this integration can become "talent." This means that for *now*, the productive relationship is a failure. The situation depends on further planning and long-term preparation—which here means an additional working area. Another and simpler way of putting this is that here the talents in question lie more in the preparatory stage of development.

(12)

One has now found a certain pattern through which one can present ideas about reality within a certain time, and one has also found a fruitful pattern that can be successfully exploited as well. The fact that a person building upon their talent to make this pattern worthwhile might also have enough room within it to express themselves obviously depends on whether the person is able to employ this talent.

One might create here an application of talent that results in renown. Only with a degree of prudence as well as the provision of a good design and workmanship can one ensure that others are able to get something satisfactory out of it. Here, there is left behind a "template" or pattern that presents itself as a complete collection with a richness that enables others to "collect themselves."

(13)

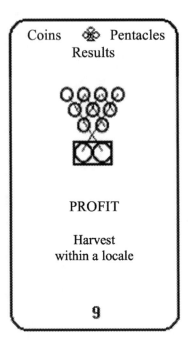

Coins   ✣   Pentacles

Results

PROFIT

Harvest
within a locale

9

When everything that one does is directed towards achieving results, this basically means that everything is about gathering a "profit." This profit is similar to the harvest, which is gathered in after the successful ripening of one's talents. Here, one is able to convert everything one can do into talents. Gathering in the profit obviously happens in a confined place in which one can enjoy it. It is like building a house as a mirror of one's own personality.

(14)

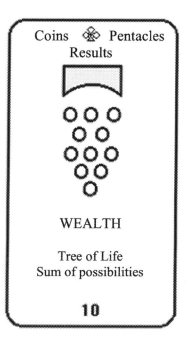

Coins ✤ Pentacles
Results

WEALTH

Tree of Life
Sum of possibilities

10

The personality is not complete until the result can be displayed or advertised everywhere. There is no need for coherence here as this stage does not have to proceed to any specific place. This is the sort of freedom of wealth that is projected towards the entire world. In itself, it is the sum of all possibilities: it is the soul that has lived and that formulates its Life and brings it to completion. To the call of the Gift, "This life I give you"—one can afterwards respond, "I lived this life."

6

THE ADDITIONS:
"TRUTH" AND "INTUITION"

According to Onno and Rob Docters van Leeuwen during the Middle Ages, in an attempt to undermine the power of its pagan images, the structure of the tarot was intentionally altered at the behest of the clergy:

> Quashing the Tarot was not an easy task for the medieval clergy because the Tarot had become widely known and used. Thus a ban by the Church would not work. The obfuscation mainly happened through *concealment* of two essential Major Arcana, followed by *changes in the order* of the remaining Major Arcana. [8]

The first of these two essential *missing cards* the van Leeuwens have called Intuition, which, according to them, takes its place in the order of the Major Arcana in a position after the Beloved (or Lovers). The second they have named Truth, and it takes its place after the card the Devil.

No longer having a place for Intuition in the organisation of our world, the flow of energy crystallises and becomes more businesslike, compromising its ability to adapt to change. Thus, we get the current interpretation of the Star of David, which actually stands for the Beloved. No longer open to intuition, a cooler, more pragmatic reasoning emerges for survival in a harsh reality. The result of such reasoning is that the outcome of developments will only evolve in one (selected) direction, which ultimately leads to an isolation of power and ultimately to a separateness. This may be inferred from the following relationship or spread:

---

[8] Docters van Leeuwen, Onno and Rob, *The Complete New Tarot* (Sterling Publishing Company, New York 2004, p. 197). Italics mine.

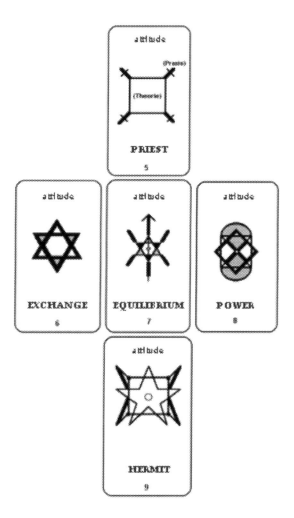

By omitting this important orientation device, the result reinforces certain determinations by emphasising a completely different arrangement. A second consequence of this is that when Intuition—understood here as openness to the complex vital logic of the interior—no longer has a place within the Whole, it will be replaced by a "point of view"—that is to say, by a personal selection leading to an increased individualism and a desire for recognition.

Onno and Rob Docters van Leeuwen offer a very different order of the Major Arcana compared with that of A. E. Waite. For the van Leeuwens, the Arcanum of the Fool is followed by the Magician, then the Priestess, the Emperor, the Beloved (or Lovers), followed by Intuition, which, in turn, is followed by the Priest, the Empress, the Chariot, the Hermit, Justice, the World Strength, the Hanged Man, Temperance, Death, the Devil, then Truth, followed by the rest of the familiar series.

From the above sequence, we can see that when Intuition follows a certain development having received freedom (from the Beloved), it then elaborates this further under a complex form of "bundled energy." As the card appearing after Intuition, the Priest could now be considered the *representative* of this energy. In this instance, having been fed by the power of Intuition, the Priest card suggests a stance indicating both magical and religious origins. Thus, the Priest originates from the open conditions following the appropriate receptivity and may just as well be called a Pagan, a Philosopher, a Mage, or a Taoist.

In later versions of tarot, however, the figure of the Priest evolved in the direction of a "High Priest" or "Pope"—that is to say, a figure who occupies a more *secluded domicile* aimed at replacing the original intuition.

Previously, the "active intuition" or *vital insight into interior processes* could be induced through certain practices under certain circumstances that would bring together the most inspiring concepts, take into account the corresponding orientations, and concentrate them into it; a method that is the very origin of all magic and religion. There once existed guidelines for the use of such "active intuition" that prevented people from identifying with their experience. Occasionally, certain identifications were permitted and deliberately actualised to temporarily represent some of these complex combinations or *inspirations*. The ancient priests knew how to dissolve the bonds of thought and let their consciousness roam free. The knowledge of how to use this "active intuition" and develop it as a means of ordering one's world has gradually become concealed. You can see the results of this distortion in the order and logic of the remaining cards in this series.

Without having a proper concept of Intuition and therefore of inspiration, the figure of the Priest becomes a kind of *representative* who has realised something that for the rest of us is either incomprehensible and superior or something "individual." All that remains for us then is to *believe* in him. Whatever he represents on this "superior level" will now depend on how much comes through him from the open condition of the Beloved. Yet since he does not act from an intuition, he may depend upon something or someone outside of it whom he is supposed to represent. Lacking the *integration of intuition,* the degree of openness of the Priest becomes *subject to control* and to a deliberate re-channelling of the energy in a different way. Needless to say, the current priestly castes may not directly "taste" all the contents of the Beloved, a fact that causes great confusion and has been the catalyst for a lengthy deviation that could have been prevented had it been made clear earlier.

According to the van Leeuwens, the second card to have been obscured in like manner is the card "Truth." The omission of this card has in turn altered further the order of the Whole. When Truth and Intuition are obscured, the self is hard to access. The *unknown* becomes shrouded in darkness. One remains in the unknown depending on what one does not know. At the same time, one remains dependent on a hierarchical structure created by those who claim to know better. The van Leeuwens suspect there was some kind of papal conspiracy lurking behind the tarot obscuration, which involved a deliberate attempt to create confusion and to consciously remove certain values so that the masses would no longer use their own intuition or even begin to know how to do so. The intentional omission of these two cards concealed a context for these values. In this way, via an incomplete tarot order in which it would be well-nigh impossible to find a context for these values, the medieval church produced a representation of their "new order of reality." Instead of a coherent working foundation, only a chaotic image would remain in which the results of a reading would inevitably fall in a manner that corresponded to the way church doctrine decreed was the "right" method of perceiving and interpreting reality. Henceforth, the consultant remains dependent upon the person with a degree of talent to make sense out of the reading. Without a proper orientation, without the necessary equilibrating elements, the complex of possibilities to be interpreted keep varying and deviating.

In this vein, it is likely that certain aspects of the hidden truth will continue to be dishonoured and will never lead to a real clarification of the situation. Moreover, there are no longer any clues with which to work and no distinctions to determine whether one is dealing with shallow associations resulting from vague intuitions or explanations that are bluffs or even lies.

Nor is there any indication that one might be fooling oneself in one's interpretation or whether something is indeed a fact arising from the logic of things themselves. In *The Fool's Tarot*, we use the cards Truth and Intuition to advance a more *directed* interpretation. For us, these additional cards can be used as "beacons" or *reference points* that assist in bringing out distinctions with regard to what really is Truth (that is to say, true, known, based on facts) and what is still Intuition (that is to say, based on interior "directions" and the interpretation of vital patterns).

The Meaning of the Card Intuition

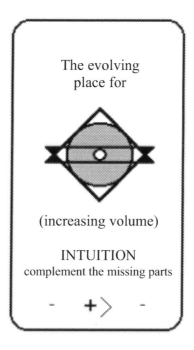

In the Tarot of the Restored Order, the card Intuition is compared with the Roman *Juno*, who rides atop a peacock. This image not only is appropriate as a symbol for the laurels of the Ego but also characterises the nature of its development: all attention and energy being drawn towards the centre.

In the above drawing, the circle represents this enlarged ego, the *inner* "volume" that is increasing or expanding and in relation to which the tension upon the environment is minimised. This means that there are very few innovative ideas present in this area that can become immediately or directly concrete and practical. This idealistic region only provides a place for things to live for (or in) themselves. It can achieve nothing in respect of existing errors as intuition is no direct incentive for truth. Here, one cannot even place truth yet (since it is new). However, Juno provides the place for change to occur from within, if experience is ready to acquire it.

In the formation of a place for new values, Intuition does not seem to be influenced by normative standards. In this area, it has a positive or stimulating effect despite the fact that the form of the place for the new values is not yet integrated. That part that is not correct is partially restored because space has been created for growth towards a solution. Thus, it stands firm in relation to this "missing future."

In the book *The Complete New Tarot*, Intuition is described as *feminine* and "negative." The choice of this association no doubt pertains to its open and receptive character and perhaps also because the female is traditionally associated with the "left" side and with the unconscious and negative pole.

In this work, however, Intuition is regarded as a force that *increases positivity* in the midst of an excess of negative tension within its area.

One cannot expect intuition to be any kind of "truth." For this reason, one could object to its bloated and impractical form. Nevertheless, its origination already works in a positive or promotional manner by making room for the things that are not there yet but which in time will take their place just as soon as we come into contact with them. Because the place of intuition is formed from the *inside*, one can learn to see what is needed for it. But before achieving a concrete result, one needs some techniques. Thus, the process of further development has to begin or nothing will come of it. All the elements it needs will start to appear in the open places and will fill in these places according to their essence. After that, they must be effectively integrated with the actual work that has only just begun. Intuition by itself only creates the right openness but not yet the discipline and work necessary to do something and make something concrete through it. Thus, it is purely alone, the favourable initial stage at the beginning of a new mode of construction.

The Meaning of the Card Truth

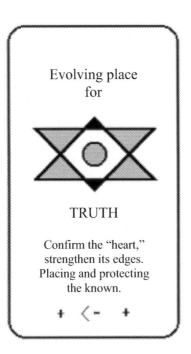

Truth, being the opposite of Intuition, tends towards the past, restoring and working from there. Its strength is that it perceives *truth in itself*. This principle recognises both what goes well and what goes awry, paying special attention to what goes wrong and can go wrong. This permits Truth to formulate laws to curtail many impossibilities. In comparison with Intuition, it is able to unmask the unrealistic expectations of excessive positivism and its lack of realistic standards. Truth stands for the *negative* in the excess of the positive.[9] It is encouraged to impose restrictions on unbalanced expansions because of unrealistic optimism or simply extensive outward growth lacking a solid foundation.

According to the van Leeuwens, Truth was formerly symbolised by Jupiter standing astride an eagle with lightning bolts in each hand. Compare these lightning bolts with the *dordje* in Buddhism—associated with truth in mental concentration or in mental discernment free of dualistic tendencies—in which the right "placing" of distinctions can break open the negative (thunderclouds) and release the power of the lightning bolt.

---

[9] The proof that Intuition is positive and Truth is negative is already noticeable in how Intuition or Truth always come across: Intuition always sounds positive and Truth negative.

In the above drawing for this card, you can recognise the shape of an eagle in the design. The truth is especially concerned with what is happening *within* Truth, with what fits within its wings—that is to say, with what one observes in the area of perception and is now becoming clearer, thanks to the magnification proceeding from the core. The origin of Truth is fashioned from the core or essence, from the sharpening of focus that occurs therein. At the core of Truth exists the "*in*-sight," which is then projected upon the wings of vision.

To this day, the Germans still regard the image of the eagle as a symbol of the State. During WWII, the German eagle received an exaggerated role as State symbol, while its opposite pole Intuition was channelled through a more ancient symbol, the Indian Swastika, which was used to replace the Christian Cross as a symbol of sacrifice. Something of this can already be seen in our earlier presentation of the order of the cards showing the transition from the Carriage (or Chariot), which is the turning wheel in this instance passing into Strength or Force, which was for the Nazis rotating in only one direction: looking to so-called facts as interpreted through the past.

Such stilted logic still hangs together with the old order following the instigation of a different value system that fits with the incomplete order of the tarot. Since the nature of Intuition was clouded by a shift in direction towards magic, the State took great care to represent a counterpart of it as well. This intuitive sensibility was able to speak as a replacement for what was considered the growth of the masses through the expression of an "exemplary leader" who pooled the energies of Strength and Power. Following the sequential order, the later card the Falling Tower became inevitable and only much later made clear the abuses and deceits of the dark side of the Force—represented by the Devil—which had been obfuscated before the card called Truth. Its effect was finally shown by the Falling Tower as that aspect of the delayed response to truth that people no longer wish to forget.

In the familiar tarot sets of today, the location of the card Intuition has been obscured from its natural position, which follows the Beloved/Lovers, suggesting that this is more specifically the card for "Trade." In *The Complete New Tarot* (The Tarot of the Restored Order), the position of the Priest has been changed and placed after the Beloved/Lovers. When we assume that Truth is an order considered to preside over a positive, progressive, linear conception of time within which economics, the index and monetary affairs are given precedence upon this world line, Intuition could only appear to be expressed as a backward movement, which, at the same time, digs for an unknown future. In this case, we do not really need to change the original order of the decks. Every original—as well as new order—can still be recognised within the same patterns providing one possesses the right understanding of its contents.

The disappearance of the card Intuition was immediately taken up and perpetuated by the Priest, who necessarily had to be associated with Intuition at the point when the card was omitted. At the same time as this deliberate change was being made, the place opposite Intuition—that is to say, the place of Truth, which follows the place of the Devil—also became obscured. Now, when Truth consciously follows the place of the Devil, one can deduct from this that it is sufficient merely to know the domain of the "shadows of things" to recognise the truth. However, when these dark sides show up more easily and the place of truth becomes obscured, the shadows of things continue the cycle and subsequently replace Truth.

When the Devil in things is not immediately converted by the recognition of Truth, its unfinished business can only be delayed and will later be captured by an aspect of the Fallen Tower.

When one looks more closely at the patterns, which are easily and logically followed, thanks to this shift, it looks as though the stock reserves of intuition and truth in our conception of society and history hasn't provided us with many benefits. Of course, here, one must see cause and effect in the correct light. It is not because of the removal of the cards Truth and Intuition that certain patterns have resulted but, rather, that this act of removal or obscuration fits very well with how *reality* has been manipulated in the modern era. If certain essentials are left out and no longer able to claim their proper context, the manner in which things are seen, related to, associated, and combined will be very different. This is, after all, how the cards themselves produce their effect. If we remove certain necessary functions from a given organism, this removal alters the coherence and the consistency of that being's logic.

On the other hand, whoever is better able to use intuition might also seek truth. The recognition of truth is a knowing that can orientate itself with the Good—as an aspect of the Lovers—as well as with Evil or the non-beneficial as in the difficult aspects and binding obligations accompanied by the shadow of the Devil. This means no longer standing outside one's own knowledge and being a slave to it because these patterns and truths now become accessible through one's personal focus. Ultimately, everything will be able to be (re)arranged according to Truth because truth is still the most logical and the most practical of functions.

But is it really true that these cards were removed at some point in history? The van Leeuwens have certainly gone to great lengths to prove that several ancient systems can be organised in an order of twenty-four cards instead of twenty-two. However, in *The Fool's Tarot*, the twenty-two cards are considered as revealing the *dependent processes* in operation, while Truth and Intuition are regarded as *useful tools* that help in the positioning of such processes and aid the process of discernment of what does and does not work restoratively to integrate the Whole.

In any case, it seems that there exists in society certain persons, groups, and organisations engaged in a course of action that is aimed at trying to arrest the processes of spontaneous growth. Such growth is dependent on natural "coincidences" in which all the elements involved are intermingled with one another in the most beneficial way. Often it turns out to be the case that there are other coordinating forces at work that consciously accelerate and decelerate certain processes (seemingly doing this with a *less visible technique of interference* that alters the direction of these forces). We must inquire as to why they do this and what they seek to achieve by doing it. For one thing, it is clear that they do this with the intention of exercising power and that they know much more about what they are doing than those who are utterly dependent on the mechanical process and are caught up in its linear illusion. It may, of course, be asked whether these exercisers of power still know the nature of what they manipulate or steer and whether they have a hidden agenda outside of this kind of influence that encourages them to remove or alter certain functions to have them fit their agenda. These are questions that arise here. What exactly the intentions are of those who intervene remains unclear. Whether they are concerned with something more than simply slowing down or accelerating events in a diagonal way is likewise unclear. What is certain, however, is that there exists a certain pull on the dynamic Whole, which is not spontaneous but comes forth from very specific and deliberately taken decisions.

Who Governs Truth?

Most of us are familiar with the Hermetic phrase "As above so below," also expressed in the Lord's Prayer as "On Earth as it is in Heaven." But behind the "As above so below" New Order of the Ages, one may suspect some subtle form of manipulation. As already mentioned, the State likes to adopt the role of the Eagle, which is quite understandable because the State likes to keep a close eye on what happens under its wings. The symbol for this is the All-Seeing-Eye (or Big Brother watching you). Quite recently, Father Yod, an American guru, made an interesting remark in relation to the *eye symbol* fashioned according to Masonic design and to be found on the back of every US dollar bill. Father Yod's remark ran something like this: "Where's the other direction in this process? Why is the opposite direction that could create a balance in this growth process not there?"

While Nazism turned its power in only one direction as a reckoning with the past, so too it would seem did the Freemasons with and through this symbol. But this is not actually the case since Freemasonry used both the symbol of Intuition—the symbol of the truncated pyramid topped by the All-Seeing Eye—as well as that of Truth or the Eagle. And in the above dollar bill, each of these symbols is to be found in their appropriate place. Yet if we really seek to use the inspiration of both these directions simultaneously to create a balanced image of mankind—as a *double triangle* referring to "trade" between persons—it may indeed have been appropriate to add this to money bills, not merely as a symbol inspiring Freedom of Trade but to promote monetary recovery and humanism through trade by using Truth and Intuition together and uniting them in one symbol. If these actually had have been used together, the symbol would have looked somewhat similar to Father Yod's design and proposition (see below) where the extra pyramid with the inverted triangle proposes Truth and the lower eye presents its tail. With an extra eye on the bottom, it would possess an eye peering from its ass (which no one needs). Yet with this double vision from above (State/Truth/Eagle) and the Freedom/Pyramid/Trade below, would it perhaps have become a better whole?

Furthermore, it must still be explained why it is that the symbol of the pyramid with one eye "inaccessible from below" also fits with the growth of Intuition. While the growth occurs from below through the increasing volume of society, the top—which is still to be integrated fully—still remains unreachable directly. According to the choices made by the generation of Freemasons after 1957, this "unknown" element became "God." This also represents the *strangers* who take control of the whole.

To the "All-Seeing Eye" of God ("In God we trust") is added the Great Seal "*Annuit Coeptis, novus ordo seclorum*," which can also be considered another confirmation of the monarchic state of money. On the other side of the dollar bill, we can see the Eagle with the motto "*E Pluribus Unum*" with the twelve stars of the former number of states continuing the theme "of the United States." This number twelve has never been modified. The number twelve, referring to the solar initiation process, is well chosen. Whether Truth and Intuition were ever deliberately removed from the context of the tarot cycle, it is clear that in the case of the United States, they were certainly given once more their own context. The question remains for the ordinary man, still subject to Chance and the Wheel of Life, whether he feels a part of this whole process and possessed of a capacity to consciously influence its evolution. The simple answer is *he is not really part of this process.*

States, religions, and other groups have precisely placed the symbols in such a way as to remain unreachable. Meanwhile, they continue to steer the overall process. However, the general tendencies of the Wheel (and of States themselves) still obey the same laws, being dependent on their evolution. Nonetheless, it is these same organisations that are defining the dynamics of the system. This begs the question, Does everything reduce to the revolutions of power? Within the secret circles, do these organisations preach power as the prior element? Seen from the perspective of a process of manipulation, power appears to be the determining factor that adds to the impact of the Wheel of Life. Yet, in reality, it only increases delays and camouflages evolutionary processes.

We may assume there exist techniques that can be consciously learned and applied to obtain greater influence over the daily pendulum of action and reaction; techniques that allow certain processes to be stimulated, accelerated or delayed; techniques of which the impact—even for those who are applying them—will not be immediately clear. Most probably, this is not even taken into account because it is in the hands of the State(s) and not of "society." Such processes pass under the form of power referred to loosely as "hidden agenda." The State itself still takes over the role of truth/law/eagle and also of intuition/inspiration/eye.

It would not be unwise to consciously incorporate these processes into the greater growth process as originally planned. Then the processes would evolve by themselves and no longer be dragged backwards. The spontaneous nature of evolution would no longer be distorted and delayed. What is presently missing is access to the next stage: *the consciousness of recovery.* This phase goes beyond the vision of power, which can only ever remain at the level of the Wheel of Life. We must learn to use Truth and Intuition *together* in the correct way—that is to say, as tools for our own orientation. Used in this way, Truth and Intuition offer the opportunity for healing, restoration, and self-recovery on all levels of our being simultaneously. And, here, the "rulers" should not be afraid that they will be completely destroyed by the introduction of such a recovery process. After all, anyone living within a natural development process will be able to continue to meet their obligations in the place where they can truly flower (and have not been forced to). The only difference is this: when that moment arrives, *all* general processes need to be followed.

With the above reflections in mind, the more complete cards Truth and Intuition appear as follows:

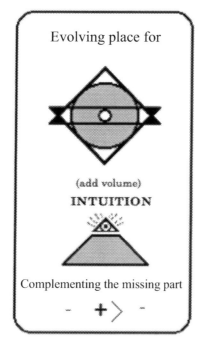

Truth may also be called the "laws" (which stand for everything that restrains us). In any case, Intuition comes forth from freedom in action—from the phase of the Lovers onwards—while Truth proceeds from the Devil onwards following conclusions arrived at after being tied to the laws. The value of reality can in fact only be increased by combining both functions in one perspective. While Intuition undertakes freely, Truth filters and arranges in a constraining fashion. Only a communicative process involving both these functions really creates something new (in terms of the next phase one is searching for). In practice, this usually means that the "something new" is the result of a recovery process.

7

READING PATTERNS

There exist a number of tarot reading patterns that make allowance for the interpretation of *reversed* cards. These types of reading patterns tend to promote opposites or polar tendencies—for example, past/future or positive/negative. As such, they are believed to provide tools that assist in the interpretation of a reading. However, these so-called aids could just as easily be deemed detrimental in that they encourage a distinctly *dualistic mode of thinking*. These types of reading patterns may also serve to accentuate a strong degree of personal projection. Perhaps a better approach to interpreting the polar function would be to consider it in terms of constructive and destructive effects within a continuously evolving process. This is certainly more true to life since all vital processes are at one moment anabolic and at another moment katabolic.

An overview of the validity and limitations of such approaches is rarely if ever included in traditional tarot books. Allowing for the stimulation of something, which may not at first glance appear to be beneficial or necessary for one's development, is often considered a "failed reading" with respect to the bigger picture. But who truly cares about the "big picture" when it comes to the usual methods? Given certain circumstances, to abort a situation may prove to be an advantageous and constructive action. The simplistic positive/negative positioning is clearly limiting and inadequate. What is missing in this enumeration of so-called useful distinctions is a recognition of the potential of many other types of dynamic movements within the tarot. For example, if we take into account the deeper nature of the involutionary-evolutionary system within the tarot cycle, we see that it allows for the possibility of motions to occur in clockwise and counterclockwise directions. By taking into account such dynamics, we can come to understand the *direction* or *purpose* of events.

Furthermore, by deploying Truth and Intuition like anchors, the Reader can come to know when an "emergent reality" can be taken in a certain direction (aided by the orientation provided by Intuition) or when to make restricted improvements (assisted by the orientation provided through Truth). Hence, *The Fool's Tarot* has been developed as a response not just to counter the excessive use and abuse of imaginative incentives but also to enable the serious Reader to properly penetrate the inner heart of the art. Necessarily, then, a new method of laying the deck imposes itself. This new method utilises Truth and Intuition as *anchors* or *arrows*. The "arrows" stretch the bow of one's personal reality to unleash it in the direction of new interpretations.

LAYING THE DECK WITH THE CARDS "TRUTH" AND "INTUITION"

A. The Two Bows Method

1) Shuffle and cut the cards in the usual manner. Make sure to shuffle thoroughly as the succession of each card counts in this method. To successfully cut and shuffle eighty cards, it is best to use a method that makes this convenient. One such method is to lay the eighty cards one by one face down on the table and then randomly reassemble them in a stack.

2) Next, comb through the deck of cards one by one until you encounter one of the two anchors—that is to say, either the Intuition card or the Truth card. Whichever one you come across first, put it down on the table. Now take at random an equal number of cards from in front of and behind your anchor card, preferably arriving at a total number of seven—that means drawing three cards *before* the anchor and three cards *after* it. We suggest the number seven because a series of seven organises itself well in the mind.

Deal the rest of the cards and lay them down in a pile until you encounter the second anchor card, which will be either Truth or Intuition. If, before encountering the second anchor, this second set of cards becomes much too large, then the deposit of cards between the two anchor points will be too many and too difficult to supervise. On the other hand, if the number within the two arches being laid down is easy to keep track of, then you may keep it visible between the two anchors (otherwise, it would require too much imagination to breach the gap between these two concepts to interpret their connections and transitions).

3) Now check which cards are lying between the Truth and Intuition Arc. These cards can be considered the consciously acquired *working material*. If there is just a handful of cards, these can be regarded as achievements and the interpretation of them accessible. Note these cards also possess a certain neutrality. If there are too many cards, it is better to leave them out of the interpretation completely because they will bring little additional insight. In this case, simply lay them in a stack between both anchors.

Just as with the first anchor card, after encountering the second anchor card, place three (or if you wish more) cards *before* it and *after* it in such a way that you can see most easily a pattern and logic.

4) The next stage is to interpret the distance you notice between Truth and Intuition. When Truth and Intuition are lying *close* to each other, this can be interpreted as being literally the case. Then the cards lying in between them and their relationships are imaginable, and the process is easy to follow. It is especially the cards *in between*, the "acquired" cards, that bring a better balance between the two arcs. However, when Truth and Intuition are *far apart*—because of the unknown character of intuition—this means that whatever is sought is not within the immediate reach of truth. In this latter case, we need to accept the condition of more unknown elements, many multiple processes, and further developments to allow for the change that is implied in intuition.

5) Next, we proceed to interpret the Truth/Intuition nexus and the surrounding cards. The cards that are placed *before* the anchor cards describe in one "sentence" the way or path to be followed, while the cards *following* them express the conclusion therefrom. The cards Truth and Intuition *themselves* describe the places where one still has an opportunity to make improvements.

The place of Truth describes the anchor point for the established facts, which the Reader already knows. By clearly articulating these facts, the Reader can control them further in moving forward.

When the Truth card comes first, the Reader has already a good perspective on the truth and can continue to move on from the facts he or she already knows.

On the other hand, if the Intuition card comes first, the truth remains hidden to some degree, and the Reader should become more open to the unknown factor(s). In this case, something has been overlooked, and the Reader needs to improve certain conditions before the truth can be perceived. An *unknown element* has yet to be recovered.

Additionally, one can turn up the previous card—that is to say, the one just *prior* to the first series of seven cards. This card can then come to represent or describe the *question* of the questioner. Also, at the end of the series, a few more cards can be added, and these additional cards will express *possible future results* that follow on from here once the truth of the (now minimum fourteen) cards lying on the table have been well worked through and understood by the Reader. One may then see much further than the presenting reality into the future with the proviso that not too many Wand cards follow because these are the cards of further change, which the Reader must still confront in a reality that has not yet arisen. Wand cards presage the confrontations that are to follow and the new kinds of situations before which the Reader will have to halt because all the events that emerge from new confrontations have not yet been established *in fact* and depend on too many issues and choices still to be made.

The reality of the fourteen cards on the table may be considered the reality of the *Present*, in the double sense of Gift/Now (see below), which is only workable as long as the Reader is doing something with it. On average, we may think of it as having an effect on future-oriented action for around three days. We can consider any *Now-Moment* as a Gift "bundled" in a similar manner. More than this, the Reader need not know. It is recommended that one try and *read* the relationship between the cards as *one sentence* so that the whole assemblage becomes clear like a simple rebus. The entire reality of the "sentence" will always be and always remain a coherent structure in which the Reader can perceive further associations and interrelationships. The fact that the two arcs or bows constrain the interpretations will force the real focus onto the laying method itself, which, just like the cards, is now directed towards finding the essential truth of something that can be grasped in terms of an *essence*.

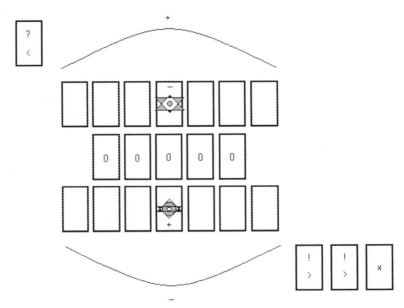

It is important to remember that when the number of cards of the middle row exceeds seven, the total card count becomes cluttered, and the content and interpretation of these cards lose their neutral capacity to connect with the ends of the two bows. When this occurs, the ballast between truth and intuition becomes over-weighted, and the Reader needs to strengthen the remaining separate connections before both aspects can work efficiently together.

If the anchoring card Truth appears as one of the first cards in the spread, it will be clear how close one is to departing from this kind of essence. If the Intuition card appears early, it indicates the *unknown* is near at hand, but its true content has been overlooked. (This is not to say that when Intuition is far away or far apart in the game that it is also far away itself). One need only look for its search conditions a little further on in the course of the game.

The advantage of this method of laying the cards is that it tests the view of reality itself to determine to what extent one has a sense for the "present reality" (or the Gift in a bundle). Of course, one still has the option of adding some cards after the facts. These additional working cards help unfold the learning process further and reveal how one may come to approach the objective facts and how later to materialise them. If at a certain point during the shuffling of the cards some cards happen to fall from the deck, these can be taken as "pointers" or reminders, which operate within the interpretation to guide one in the perception of the correct direction.

B. The Board with Eighty Places

Since it is difficult and sometimes even impossible to shuffle eighty cards effectively, one can construct a board with eighty places on which to distribute a reading. After shuffling the cards well, one can more easily place the cards one by one on the board. An example of such an order of eighty is shown below:

past/conditioned situation

present concrete situation,
which remains under control ->

to do/still to make/
to deal with/becoming

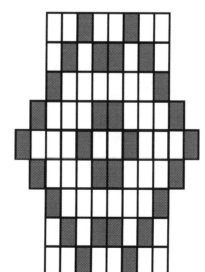

1) Place the cards face down on the board. As an option, one may turn over a random card, which can serve to represent the question or the concern of the querent.

2) Now look for the anchor cards Truth and Intuition. Having discovered them, one can turn them over and make them visible.

3) Next, turn over an equal number of cards lying close by. This means turning over three cards *before* and three cards *behind* each of the anchors. As before, these cards indicate "what comes *from*" and "what leads *to*"—"before" and "after" can be a number between zero (when the anchor card comes

first) and seven cards. The cards "before" and "after" can represent the *past* and the *future* (before and after the conclusions). Each additional card may, of course, provide further detail, but, remember, one need not go too far here and pick out a large number of cards even though it may be helpful sometimes to penetrate deeper into clarifying the basic pattern one has initially laid down.

When the Intuition card appears first, this means that the *unexpected*, the *unprecedented*, the *unknown*, and also *what is still to be formed* prevails. On the other hand, when the card Truth appears first, there is a *dominance* (or domination) of *incurred and truly known facts*. It remains the case that it is easier to use seventy-eight cards for creating a regular pattern. This is so because with a series of eighty, it is immediately apparent that the two additional cards cannot but operate in a coordinating role.

C. The Past-Present-Future Method

To place a past-present-future reading orientation within the parameters of a simple linear timescale is incomplete. The linear scale is dependent on a two-dimensional thought process. Thus, one cannot take into account other kinds of developments, learning processes, or inclinations that have different rhythmic temporal patterns. What we are really stating here is that past-present-future interpretations can and must be approached differently.

To do so, we need to approach such interpretations with a different understanding of time and evolution. For the particular method of past-present-future interpretation being proposing here, we need to lay out three rows of cards. Each row will be composed of a pattern of five cards. Four of these five cards we place in a cross form, and the fifth or middle card will be the card used to orientate the Reader. In the case of the first five cards, the *middle* card represents what one has to put up with or "endure."

The "past" equates to all that has passed, to what one has passed over, to what one has met with, as well as to what is bound to patterns. For example, when someone dreams about things associated with their parental home, such dreams are usually about associations that bind that person to what they have learned or received. In such cases, it is better not to lay the main emphasis of this directly on the "I" (as the representative of self-consciousness) because the person can have been affected by things that the "I" does not even possess. The further back into the past one probes, the more it appears others have provided the values to one's life. Sometimes, such values correspond to who one "really" is, but very often they do not.

The word "present" in both English and French has two meanings: the sense of "now" as in the present time and also the sense of "gift" as in a birthday present. The *Gift* is exactly what you are being offered *Now*. Now (the vital moment) is always a Gift (something given). Only you can decide whether to do something with the gift. The present moment can be controlled from and oriented by the past, or it can be what will determine how the future will look. The interpretation of the combinations that are formed around the present are forming the present as well. A second row of five cards represent this phase in which the middle card is the "gift" (or potency).

The "future" is what is reserved for what serves one. It is the rediscovery of the true self. Therefore, it does not have to lie in the future. It is logical to evolve towards it; otherwise, one might lose control over oneself and one's life. It is envisaged *to exit* in the future. Five more cards represent this third aspect. The middle card in between is the "guiding principle" for this.

In total, this gives fifteen basic cards (three series or patterns composed of five cards each):

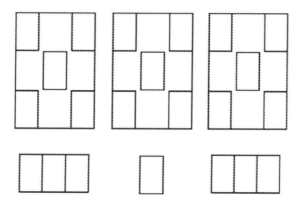

In the above diagram, we see the Past-Present-Future reading pattern of twenty-two places. The upper pattern of fifteen cards has already been explained. Now we must give our attention to the extra row of seven cards beneath, which we find expressed the real-time directive for the Past-Present-Future reality.

After grasping what one has understood from the past and what one can or would want to use from the future, one can lay a few more cards beneath these fifteen basic cards to re-evaluate the interpretations, only this time within a real time frame. As a matter of choice, this can be done either with a new reading, which will reuse all the cards together, or, more directly, as a dependent vision, which uses some of the remaining cards. Once again, this is best expressed through the use of seven cards. When one has made the choice to add these seven extra cards to the already established pattern, it is best to keep these extra cards face down until one has interpreted the preceding fifteen cards.

Three of the cards in this new lower series represent the past. The first card represents what one has been given, the second card represents the potential, and the last card what one has managed to make from it up until now. The card in the middle of the lower row is the current primary reality and situation. The following three cards are about the future.

As an option, one may read the cards in terms of twenty-four places instead of twenty-two. The extra places, left and right, can still be added as a sort of guide to see how one has been helped through the past, with what kind of energy, and how this will be assisted further in the future and how it might be achieved.

8

THE PROCESSES OF RECOVERY
IN THE MAJOR AND MINOR ARCANA

As an example of how the process presently under way may be developed further, let us turn our attention to the underlying dynamics of restoration. The initial cycle of twenty-two cards follow a pattern that appears to inhibit the process of recovery. From here onwards, however, we can consciously choose to engage this process. Below is a scheme revealing the basic structure of this process.

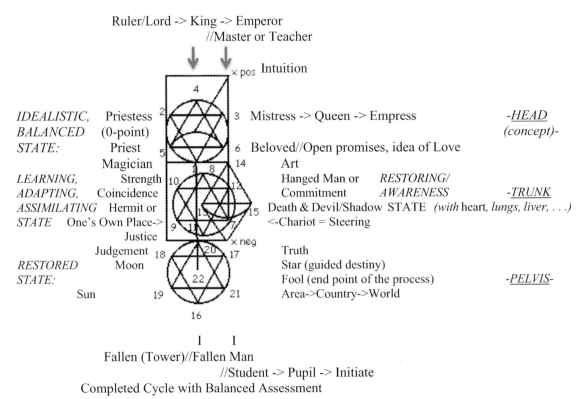

Ruler/Lord -> King -> Emperor
//Master or Teacher

x pos Intuition

IDEALISTIC,   Priestess   3 Mistress -> Queen -> Empress   -HEAD
BALANCED   (0-point)   (concept)-
STATE: Priest   6 Beloved//Open promises, idea of Love
               Magician   14   Art
LEARNING,   Strength   Hanged Man or   RESTORING/
ADAPTING,   Coincidence   Commitment   AWARENESS   -TRUNK
ASSIMILATING   Hermit or   15 Death & Devil/Shadow STATE (with heart, lungs, liver, . . .)
STATE   One's Own Place->   <-Chariot = Steering
               Justice
               Judgement 18   Truth
RESTORED   Moon   17   Star (guided destiny)
STATE: Fool (end point of the process)   -PELVIS-
         Sun   19   21   Area->Country->World

        16

I   I
Fallen (Tower)//Fallen Man
//Student -> Pupil -> Initiate
Completed Cycle with Balanced Assessment

In the second volume of *The Fool's Tarot*, the complete construction of this path will be explained in greater detail along with the movements necessary to "walk" it via its lunar (4) and solar (10) rhythmic processes, the 4 x 14 different stations of the Minor Arcana and their cycles: daily for the Sun, monthly for the Moon, and via the quaternary phases of the Seasons. The above scheme only shows the inhibited processes (or that what "is"). Later on, we shall see how the practice of this scheme via the Major Arcana will assist us in dealing with the outside directions of change and what *to do*.

One can, however, already see how the processes of the Major Arcana can be divided into the initial four stages of awareness. In the Head Centre, one begins with an idea or ideal of the world (the idealistic balanced state indicated above). By means of the Intuition-Truth axis, one eventually finds a ground by means of which one can learn to assess what exactly can and cannot be made in the daily processes and what tends to remain in the dark in each process. The second state, which refers to the state of learning, adapting, and assimilating within the body, pertains to the human trunk, where everything is digested and processed directly and is grounded by the Life Cycle itself.

The next circle can be seen to be out of balance, away from its centre, starting a process with (and from) the same (rhythmical) ratios, as a real-life test that checks its practical implications and must be worked out in relation to the theoretical reality, with its fit processes of coincidence, Justice, Steering, and Strength. Here, the theory is projected into action. The resulting differences will be felt via the third part (triangle 13-14-15), which will be experienced as negative imbalances within the next stage of the processes that already include a first feedback with restorative awareness. When the gap between theory and practice had been large or significant, this ought to indicate a significant residue relating to Death (or disease) or the Devil (increased shadows in the materialisation process). The card Judgement (20) introduces the last cycle, where the amount of false reality and its feedback to it will once again be adapted to the ideal practical reality (guided by the Moon and the Star and inspired by the Sun and the World). These will reveal the true processes that ought to be adapted at each moment.

A large amount of these ongoing developments described here in the awareness processes of the Major Arcana could make adaptation difficult. However, a person who has understood the underlying dynamics of this kind of learning process can work directly in an undeviating line of development (0–22), almost like a "spine," without having to undergo many of the inhibiting recovery stages that concern one's general adaptation. There is a requirement to adapt to the needs of a basic condition while facing the notion that the world itself will reveal the extent of practical limitations. These difficult stages, in what is a very direct learning process, expose the necessity and importance of adapting one's attitude to it. In this respect, the Fool—if this card is indeed the last card and actually stands for the twenty-second stage or state of awareness and is not, as some systems seem to suggest, the perspective of the World—will be able to *oversee* this cycle directly and use the starting point of the recovery processes immediately from the start. At this point, one will then stand "outside" or "beyond" the cycle while still depending on the initiative of its environment and what the world has to offer.

It is also possible to compare this scheme with a process of activation developed through an order of seven, which operates somewhat like a Western-based system of chakras. Again, this system will be examined in greater detail in volume 2. For now, we will only say that from the point of view of the "Western mentality," where the *process of change* is more apparent, it is important to be *active* and engage oneself in a process of restoration through *action*. Thus, the activation of a process of awareness will be put in motion after the realisation of what one needs to *do*.

Of course, certain processes exist that pass through this initiation more directly. One can also be trained in such a way as to adapt to such an approach. A directly felt intuitive relationship that incorporates the energy encompassing all the processes that can be seen here might express itself in a sort of "religious experience" of awareness. The dependency of the *overview* in this case always begins from the Hangman's position. Like the Kabbalah teaches different levels of influence and interpretation, the same processes with which to experience this can also lie on different levels of influence. Where the Emperor represents the overview itself, the learning process in its realistic developments should place at this juncture a teacher. The pupil will then represent the dependent energy to this aspect of the process. In this way, the stimulating balance between a growing love for truth will bring about a willpower of potentials into the life stream. Further variations of such forms of teaching processes will again be explained in greater detail in volume 2.

Once a pupil actively commits him or herself to change and the recovery process inhibited in the Major Arcana has begun its process, various forms of spontaneous developments begin to emerge. The most common sort of awareness process starts initially in the heart. From there, it becomes a mental inspiration. Finally, steps are taken to assimilate it instinctively.

If one fails to follow this process consciously and leaves it to develop only spontaneously, one will still be led by a distinctly mental intuitive process, which will eventually find its experience, and effectively integrate there what it discovers. Such a dependent maturation process corresponds with the processes that can be discovered and stimulated through working with the tarot.

What is most important to remember at this point is that there exist ways and means of *filling the gaps* as soon as we learn to be open to the unknown factor that completes its lack of perspective. At this stage, it is crucial to maintain an open awareness towards the process of change so that one's attention secures what is necessary to sufficiently integrate what is required at all times. This new kind of practical attention (plus intuition) provides the basis for a process by means of which one is able to increase the degree of openness and through which one becomes capable of assimilating the past and integrating its unfinished processes in relation to the future. The next chapters will reveal the underlying processes of assimilation and the processes required to thoroughly integrate certain dualities as well as possible syntheses, which must be established before the fused open processes provide us with new ways of understanding and will show us how the totality of all circumstances guides us.

9

THE THIRD ARCANA
AND THE INTERNAL DYNAMICS
OF THE GRAND SCHEME

We already have been focusing on learning the meaning and significance of the cards Truth and Intuition. So long as these two fail to harmonise with one another, the need remains for a practical method to bring about their coordination. Such coordination can be developed and deepened through the work of the Third Arcana. However, before we turn our attention to explore the inner nature of the Third Arcana, let us first review the "dualities" that have in the meantime developed and taken shape through the evolution of the processes in the tarot.

If everything was perfect or perfectly understood, one would experience no duality. It is due to imperfection that a development process is enacted. Such a development process we may call here "the long way round" as opposed to the *immediate synthesis*. Yet the development process (or "long way round") provides a path that, when summarised and successfully adapted to, can still bring distinction.

The 0-Fool and the 22-Fool or Joker

As anyone who is even remotely familiar with an ordinary pack of cards should know there are two Jokers or two blank cards included in every deck. These cards perform a role in the standard playing deck similar to the role the cards Truth and Intuition perform in the tarot—that is to say, they are important for purposes of orientation although not *directly* involved in the game. When one adds these two cards to the deck and understands how to integrate them into the system, a certain order becomes clear because their inclusion allows for the observation of *two opposite directions* within a single evolution.

One can regard the two kinds of Joker as representing two types of people: those who realise the Wheel of Life and those who do not. The latter kind of Joker remains dominated by the forces of the First Arcana, whereas the former kind of Joker is the one who learns to adapt his attitude to the Rules of the Game. This Joker (22) is the Joker or Jester who laughs with life because he has passed through the various phases and has understood everything. Yet even this Joker remains only a particular kind of Fool. It is this consciousness that prompted Gurdjieff to probe his students time and again with the provocation, "Know the kind of Fool you tend to play."

Within the Wheel of Life and its events, it is more important to know what kind of fool you are than to know what kind of master. The reason for this is that a master can only be fully a master in *one* of the twenty-two phases, while a fool is able to adapt continuously to all sorts of phases and feels no compulsion to enforce anything. One can better divide this sort of Fool who is not really a Joker since a Joker is basically only one general attitude that aims to lighten the situation into two major types.

The first type is the 0-Fool, who lives from intuition and is completely open and free and lives like a nomad or a gypsy. The problem with this type of Fool is that he or she cannot intervene in a situation but remains totally dependent on circumstances. Consequently, fate cannot be reversed for such a person. The 0-Fool is profligate and irresponsible but experiences much.

The 22-Fool is just the opposite. This Fool lives on the familiar, on what he or she knows, and thus is severely limited. This Fool's attitude is one of *choice*. He or she quickly takes on the characteristics of a magician or a controller.

Both Fools are extremes and can be viewed as the Yin/Yang aspects of the changing reality propelled by the Fool. On the one hand, the 0-Fool cannot adjust the conditions; on the other hand, the 22-Fool is capable of manipulating circumstances. Both attitudes are follies, which by themselves will not improve reality. To truly take responsibility for the whole and for the development of ourselves and the environment, it is necessary to adopt an attitude that adapts easily. This attitude is already beginning to take place in the First Arcana through the emphasis on adopting the correct attitudes amidst the twenty-two available options. Adapting and adjusting properly to this predetermined and erroneous process of manipulation will not occur until we experience more fully the processes of the Third Arcana via these same twenty-two cards. In it, the stance of the Fool keeps a place outside the whole so that there are in fact only twenty-one cards of direct influence, or 3 x 7 + 1.

The "dualities" encountered in the evolution of the first twenty-two cards are like the sum of the differences between Fool-0 and Fool-22, otherwise known as Jokers 1 and 2 (comparable in a sense to knowing Truth and using Intuition). From the perspective of these two poles, the Fool-0 is seeking to lighten affairs, while Fool-22 is forever making things heavier. The Joker in his role as Jester works to unravel the underlying situations while playing and making extra opportunities for later choices. Truth and Intuition as direct inspirations can therefore consciously alter the process-related issues by making them lighter or heavier.

Level 1 of this 0–22 dualism is experienced by the Fool as a *physical* appearance, level 2 is experienced as *instinctive* confrontation for the Joker, level 3 is experienced as *astral* (being the first step for consciously using Intuition), and level 4 is *mental* (being the first step for mobilising Truth). The next and last level is engaged with fate or searching for the soul's destiny—a very different way of dealing with things. Here, nature and natural balance seek to regain the upper hand.

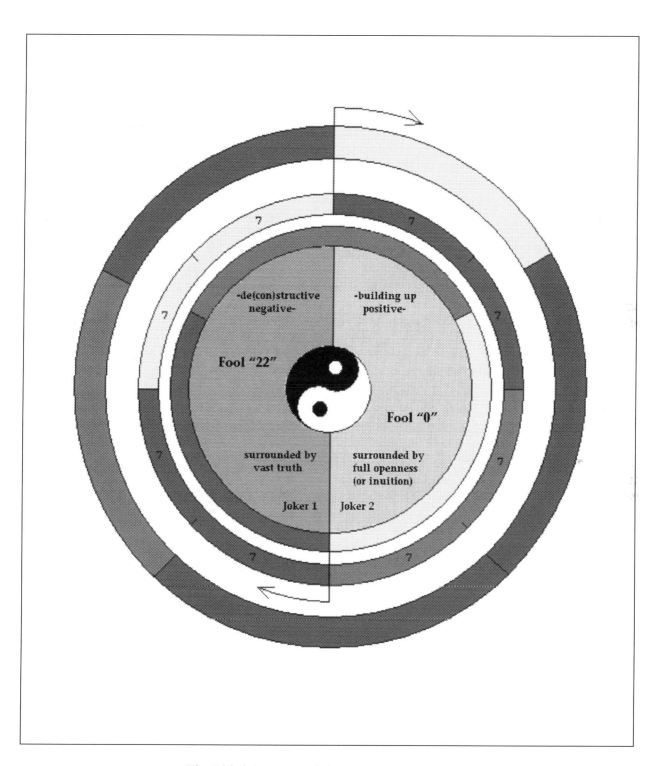

The Third Arcana and the Evolution of Colours

The Deviant Stance: The Magician

The separation of Tao or the Unity of Being into Fool (unconscious) and Joker (conscious) creates a centre of *personal choice*. In one sense, this is the choice to create something that will necessarily undergo a process of re-integration. As one begins to learn and recognise one's own choice in this process, one begins to realise that this choice is *Not Tao*. The essence of this conscious choice, which appears to originate from the centre of the Magician, is rooted in a summation of the dualism emerging between the two poles of the Fool. Man feels himself to be a magician and creator of life, while in fact his life and being are characterised by foolishness. Every so-called magician is subsequently dependent on a process that is put into motion through Tao in twenty-one successive phases.

At some point, the question surfaces as to what really constitutes the starting point of an evolution: the Fool or the Magician?

As we have already said, man imagines himself to be a magician, while in essence he is a fool. The *authentic* Magician (used as a new centre of origin) is actually the *overview of the whole system*, a state of being that only becomes fully active at the 111th phase, when the complete system of development ceases and the overview can be seen. However, the magician at the beginning of each new process initiated is something entirely different.

One can assume the magician posture and pretend to control the evolution whilst displaying an air of importance. Yet this pretence acts against the general evolution and becomes ensnared once more in a particular perspective, which will make itself known in a new and predetermined unfoldment. It is through the adoption of this arrogant attitude that makes choices based on limited "truths" that such personal development is set in motion. When one recognises the position of the Fool in one's own choices, one realises that limited "truths" represent the automatism inherited from previous processes, which have now been activated. If one permits oneself to be instinctively led by the Fool, one can facilitate the necessary progression and learn to experience the beginning and end points of any phase of development.

One can deviate from the path and continue in complete unconsciousness without having altered anything. This is the Gurdjieff view of man "asleep." Or one can become conscious and learn to follow the process *actively*. In the latter case, one can use one's increasing awareness to form syntheses, which expand the level of one's perception until finally one is able to place oneself beyond this personal evolution—that is to say, outside its limited position—keeping, henceforth, an overview of the circumstances one encounters. If one finds oneself confronting time and again various kinds of challenging circumstances, it is most likely the case that one has remained ensconced in the condition of the arrogant and pretentious magician who in essence remains a fool.

It is much wiser to experience "All and Everything" like a Fool and learn how one's automatic reactions can be one's teachers. After attaining consciousness of the automaton, the next step is to obtain the vision of the *Overview*.

Through the Gift of the Overview, we learn to make syntheses, which combine different levels of awareness. Only the Overview can break down the forces of action and reaction inherent within the automaton. Eventually, the turning of the wheel and its processes dominate one less and less. To get a sense of what we mean by the term "Overview," it is necessary to understand something of the internal dynamics of the Grand Scheme.

The Internal Dynamics of the Grand Scheme

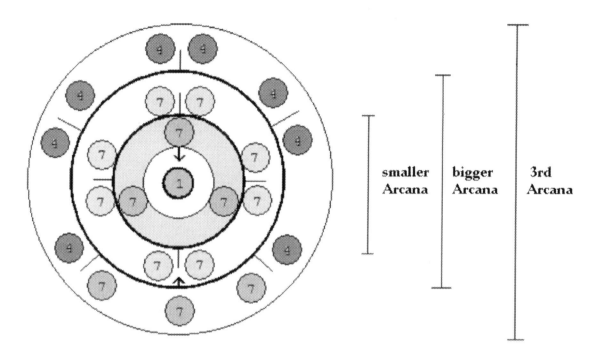

The starting point (Point 1) located in the *centre* of the diagram above depends on the degree of attention present in the current moment and the determination of its effect. Moving out from the centre to the next numbered circle, we meet the First or Major Arcana (the 21 or 7/7/7), which reveals the impact of this starting point. Its further development consists of three phases: development (or exploitation), impact (or confrontation), and result. Next, we have the Second or Minor Arcana (the 56 or 7/7-7/7-7/7-7/7) through which there occurs an increase of attention towards the process of development, thanks to an experiential focus on the four sensory bodies and their spontaneous interactions. The outermost ring, or Third Arcana (the 32 incorporating the 21), is fully adapted to the process of *necessity* where the participant becomes the being who is independent of all three cycles. The twenty-one general stances are now given the *neutral position* that is required in the sort of situation where each phase in the cycle refers to a similar phase within the four sensory bodies. This is represented as 4 x (4 + 4), or 32 places that relate to each other and are enriched by a fully nourished consciousness as twenty-two neutral places that have fully adapted to the situation.

The above scheme proposes the following divisions:

- the division of 1 (Tao or the blank card), which when put into motion through a process, becomes either the Magician or the Fool according to perspective;
- the division into 2, the two Jokers, which in this case are two types of Fool: the conscious Fool (akin to a magician) and the unconscious fool (lacking awareness);

- the division into 3, providing the twenty-one general attitudes (+ 1, the Fool) all lacking consciousness;
- the division into 4, which gives the four centres and their fourteen stages of development (represented as 2 x 7 in dualistic modes);
- the division into 5 with the twenty-one positions (+ 1 as a conscious summary of the Major Arcana) with the addition of the thirty-two intelligences acquired through merging processes in which the participant becomes free from learning processes or blockages via enhanced consciousness.

All together, these give rise to 21 + 1 + 56 + 32 + 21 + 1 = 132 distinct stages in total. Truth and Intuition as intermediaries are not included. Twenty-two places appear twice and are second time around mostly reorientations. Thus, we have only 110 phases that constitute the complete actual learning process.

If one looks at the current proportions in which all the various aspects are self-organising, one gets slightly different ratios because the Minor Arcana are formed of 4 x 4/10 rather than the expected 4 x 7/7. Here, also, the Third Arcana of thirty-two "parts" splits itself into different ratios. Later, we will look more closely at the order of these ratios of the Third Arcana. In the meantime, we must first understand how the scheme proceeds logically to the third part:

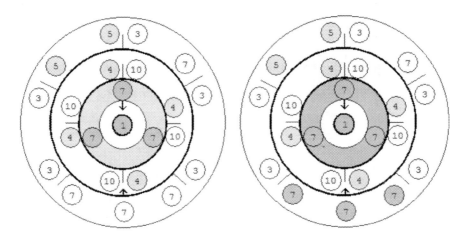

The first time one passes through the Major Arcana, the subdivisions of 3 x 7 are not at first sight apparent. However, in this study, it will soon become clear how these relationships are determining for this cycle. It is also important to be clear from the outset about the distribution of the Minor Arcana into four phases prior to the forming of each element. These we now know to be the four human figures of the King, the Queen, the Knight, and the Page followed by the numerical sequence Ace through to 10. The Third Arcana or thirty-two Paths of Wisdom already reveals the familiar division into 3, 7, 10, and 12. Through this scheme, we will come to appreciate the dynamism of these underlying relationships.

The fundamental Major Arcana remains 21 + 1 (or 22). The Minor Arcana is now 4 x 4 and 4 x 10 (or 4 x 14). The Third Arcana contains 4 x 3, 2 x 10, or 2 x 5 = 10, and 7 and 3 (and 21 + 1). This last Arcana concerned with recovery and coordination does not give a perfect five-angular distribution because the underlying proportions and distributions are more dynamic than regular.

In the scheme below, we now find added the different colours for the four centres of experience:

118

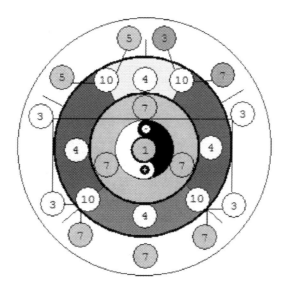

This layout gives us a total of twenty-two or twenty-four divisions. Note that when counting the position of the Fool, it is not necessary to expose its dual form. Note, too, that all divisions of the first two Arcana together with the inclusion of the position of the Fool show exactly twelve positions, revealing once more the dependency of these two Arcana on the twelvefold rhythmic cycle. Another rhythmic alternation to pay attention to here is how the outer scheme is ordered by arrangements of 4, 3, and 2, whilst other sections are governed by orders of 4, 3, 2/1. These arrangements are in no way contrived. Later, you will see how these structures and their order have a purpose and a content that fits with this order.

The scheme presented here only shows one direction of evolution; whereas, there are in fact two directions. The first direction of evolution is quite simply the one produced by an individual's own personal activities, interpretations, and reactions; whilst the *reverse* or *complementary direction* proposes the evolution that still needs to be acquired. When we add the symbols associated with the four centres of experience (hearts, spades, clubs, and diamonds), we get the following two schemes:

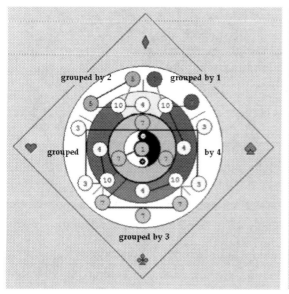 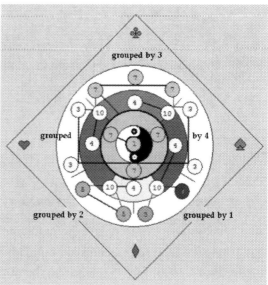

On the first scheme (above left), you can see uppermost in this cycle the symbol of the diamond (or rhombus), indicating the instinctive orientation or survival instinct to become. On the opposite pole/evolutionary trend, we find the practical symbol of the club as the chief inspiration. When we bring together the two directions, the overall scheme (presented without the numbers) looks something like this:

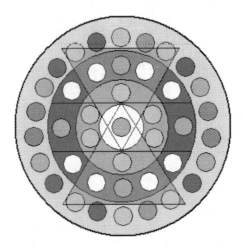

We may now compare this scheme with another scheme presented by Aleister Crowley in relation to the Kabbalah:

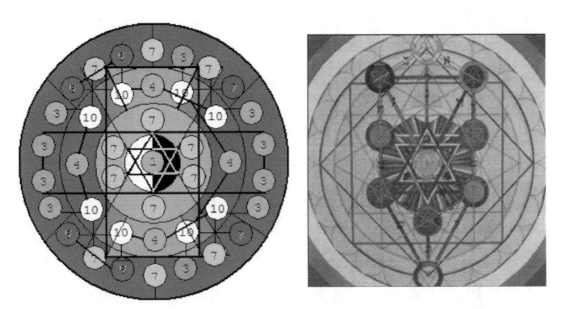

In Crowley's Kabbalistic scheme (above right), one of the intersections is not marked. It will become clear in the working out of the Third Arcana that this particular point representing the sphere *Daat* or "Knowledge" will only become accessible or responsive after the completion of a full cycle.

What we may have considered amiss in our earlier presentation was the indiscriminate merging of the two directions of evolution. We now see that the reverse evolution must still be made and therefore must remain *open*. Thus, we get the following (more realistic) adaptation:

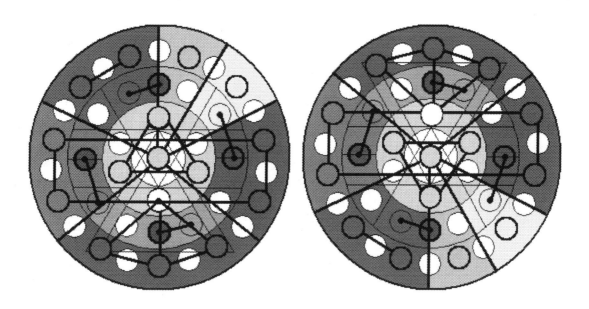

The final scheme summarising all that happens in the complete evolution of the three Arcana is to be found on the front cover of this book and will appear later again in our final study of the Third Arcana.

10

THE TRANSCENDENT TEN

Once we are able to view the twenty-two stances in a state of balance with the needs of the moment, both in terms of our *outer attitude* corresponding to the Major Arcana as well as from *within* corresponding to the Minor Arcana, we will then be able to function at a higher level, and our attention may be given to more extensive combinations. For this to occur, the individual states have to be more or less in balance. To clarify the relationship between the three Arcana, we have constructed the scheme below, which takes into account the different phases or distinct sequences to be found in each Arcana.

The Starting Point for the First Ten New Centres of Awareness

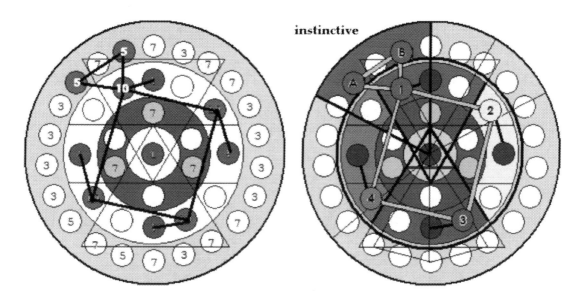

instinctive

The Transcendent 10   **The Transcendent 10**

This new phase commences after one has passed through the last phase of the full series pertaining to the *instinctive* learning process. Here, again, one clarifies all the experiences gathered from the four centres and begins to place these experiences in correspondence with one another. Before one is able to convert the sum of experiences and conclusions passed through into a "synthesis," one must first have gained insight into the practical state of each phase and know how to employ it if needed in each stage. Hence, this new kind of division and its ten phases proposed as enhanced pairings. Thus, we have ten phases in which all four centres will be experienced simultaneously on the same level at the same time. This results in the following series of ten stages within which an equal number of "intelligent paths" are released or opened up.

What happens here is the mobilisation and purification of an instinctive manner of dealing with a full synthesis of four centres of experience able to open themselves up to the full reality of the world. The emergence of the advantages and disadvantages resulting from the simultaneous experience of the four centres releases the first guiding intelligence: the "Mystical Intelligence." This intelligence simply and naturally brings together the elements of inspiration through the correct base "setting" alone without the need for power or any kind of forcing of circumstances. The spontaneous emergence of this ability is initially prepared through an "openness," which simply attends to the needs of each moment even though one may not "know" what to do from a rational point of view. Here, all the senses work together in detecting the correct budding points or conditions that allow for full commitment. Through the assistance of the process concerned with defining the "truth"—by means of which one is prepared to see "truth" at the *vital moment*—there is formed an area of neutrality, a space of "knowing" wherein one finds a balance between the openness for truth and the determination to recognise it.

The intelligence that develops from here attains results that, from the point of view of ordinary logic, cannot be explained. One receives insights because one *is* where one ought to be. One sees things in their proper perspective because one is focused on learning to evaluate situations appropriately. The initiative that extends from here develops into a state of inspiration through the processes involved. This *new inspiration* corresponds to joint control over the four Aces, which together establish a balanced orientation within the four centres of experience. Now, one knows how to observe experiences in a *neutral way* without any need for manipulation.

The resulting actions provide a sense of illumination and a sense of "knowing what to do." One's sensibility in this stage is sincere, so much so that each effect that occurs appears as perfectly adequate. One also knows where improvements may be sought and whence one may draw the necessary discernment. One also knows where the energy is finalised and purified in its true essence and how it leads to a credible form which stands up to scrutiny.

An Extra Orientation within the Third Arcana and Its Thirty-Two Parts

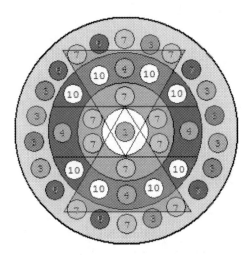

All the experiences in the previous Arcana have been different in nature. The twenty-two cards of the Major Arcana were divided into phases of 7, which one can consider the direct experience of relationships within nature and within one's own being. They are *ratios*, which appear always and everywhere in equal proportion. In one sense, the Major Arcana is subject to a random multitude of confrontations of form, colour, and sound and possesses a limited capacity to recognise the proportionate order of its own cycle.

The Minor Arcana, on the other hand, is able to anticipate the factor of coincidence that occurs within it through its *shared* learning processes. This "middle" or mediating Arcana with its fifty-six positions is distributed over twelve places.

The Third or "Completing Arcana" has twenty-two positions on the outside of the scheme and also thirty-two paths (or "Rulers") of which the first ten phases are the result of a simultaneous equilibrium among the four centres and their four kinds of learning processes: mental, emotional, instinctive, and practical.

The Third Arcana as Process of Recovery

Many of the processes expressed in the Major Arcana could attain completion in everyday life and thereby put into perspective the relativity of the ego. Yet it is also possible to fall back into the confusion that control over these processes is still related to personal achievement, to ideas of power and control, or to the notion that further results might be acquired through them.

At this point, it is not yet certain that the Joker has been inspired from the side of service to the Whole, or that the Magician who comes forth from the process of development is the controller or manager of Necessity—precisely for the reason that these roles will be defined more thoroughly during the next process. It will then become increasingly clear who or what the real guiding intelligences behind everything are and also what attitude one has been manifesting up until that point—that is to say, whether it has been spontaneously formed from automatisms, deliberately fashioned from power, or already oriented and open to recovery.

For those who want to proceed in terms of *power*, the Third Arcana appears like "magic." However, a sound psychological basis should remain recognisable behind it. While a mental capacity to recognise patterns in situations remains active, what increases a deepening of this talent is what can increase the intelligence within it. With "magic," this is not the case. It will only continue to fixate on the correct positions themselves and therefore will integrate less of the inspiring forms. For this reason, a person who aims to finish the process in a more technical sense will need to pay increasing attention to larger scales and points of balance.

The greater insight that comes from a truly lived and shared experience at all levels will eventually emit an enhanced radiance. The entire field of perceptions becomes larger and reveals a greater sense of responsibility. At this point, every situation one encounters no longer looks like coincidence. One ceases to feel oneself a plaything of circumstance. The extensive synchronicity that comes into play at this juncture makes things fit properly simply because this is its inherent aim.

Releasing the thirty-two types of Intelligence also makes possible an improvement to the "base mentalities," which benefits the whole. During the process of awareness, these "mentalities" will develop more thoroughly into viable talents through various circumstances. Only in the thirty-third stage—that is to say, the stage of the recognition of the "complete steering principle," will it become clear what this activity is making possible, what it can and cannot achieve, and which processes can be promoted or extended depending on the needs of its elements. Following the processes of the Minor Arcana, which were still subject to circumstances, this initial phase of renewal works as follows:

The first phase or first step expresses itself here as a renewal through a new kind of impersonal attitude that permits one to remain stable with an unprecedented confidence, uninfluenced by anything or anyone. One is able to maintain this attitude in all circumstances because one has previously created a form of equilibrium, which now orients the four centres of experience and their fully engaged essences or capacities *simultaneously*. This attitude of "holding all the Aces" only becomes clear following proper preparation and combination of the four Aces of the four parts of the Minor Arcana. The Questor, who has experienced all of these in all of their aspects, will now be able to recognise these potentials anywhere.

Path 1: The "Mystical Intelligence"

By combining all that has been consciously experienced whilst establishing each of the four Aces, a new form of openness of experience is established. The initial Path of Intelligence concerns (mentally) the recognition of what really does and does not concern one (emotionally) as a perspective, the discovery of one's own purpose in life (instinctively), what potentials one becomes easily familiar with, and, last, how these aspects are all becoming (practical) for one. This totality forms the useful procreative attitude towards its points of understanding in its own specific style. In this way, what comes more naturally forms also more natural connections and conditions to attract new elements and solutions. The way in which these new additional elements are found is an automated process of making new connections that cannot be explained from the position of individual control over the additions in the situation. One collects new elements in a way that is sensed, accessed, and collected instinctively.

The newly emerged mode of intelligence with its ability to discriminate and put new things into its "own perspective" provides insights that arise from a certain "maturity." With the new essence that is formed, one can take sufficient distance from the given circumstances so that conclusions are not coming from an assemblage of personal knowledge but are guided by a discovery process that comes forth from the elements that are gathered by themselves. It simply assembles what its current position and circumstances have managed to gather and "mature from somewhere." The results unfold as the sum total of help and inspiration (from outside) allied with one's own attainments (from within), which together form a "ground" for new *unknowns*.

In the study of the Thirty-Two Paths by Rabbi Akiba Ben Joseph, they call the achievement of this state "the First Sparkle" and associate it with the Sphere of "Kether" (the Crown) on the Kabbalistic Tree. Of the Sphere Kether, it is said no one can penetrate the first essence or know from whence it truly comes. This may be one of the reasons why the liberation of new understandings connected with this phase is called the "Mystical Intelligence."

Thus, to partake of the pips and "be the very essence of the cards" is to partake of an intelligence that knows how to stay alert to everything one encounters and is able to sense in advance the direction in which everything is going or where it may wish to proceed henceforth. This achievement is largely intuitive in composition and cannot be learned through any theory. For example, a mentor in a roundtable situation would discover the essence of an additional force or impetus emerging from the direction in which a conversation was developing, which he could then distil and draw from without having any personal interest in doing so. The mediating element in our roundtable example is less important than the "sensing" aspect that detects where confrontations may occur and how we might continue with them afterwards. Here, we discover the "basic terrain" of feelings. Remember that, technically speaking, the area of feelings always concerns the potential interactions possible between people. One senses here what could help make such kinds of interaction stronger. At the same time, the rational mind focuses on being conscious of its "own place," ensuring that one reinforces "one's own attitude" and that this is done with clarity. One also takes care to make correct choices among the results assembled so that one may do something that is specifically useful. Somehow, one just knows how one is best able to achieve things. Yet the nature of this intuitive perception cannot be explained. All one can tell is that the budding point for such objectives is powered by the essences from which they are built.

How one manages to distinguish all these elements involves the simultaneous interaction of all four centres: mental, emotional, instinctive, and practical. This unified Intelligence becomes a "transcendent talent" because it can change situations *in their essence* by acting on the potentials that become visible and manageable. To understand and develop this talent further, one requires another kind of intelligence that can give consequence to the first rather than simply recognising it. But to know and recognise our starting point does not yet create a complete interaction. After the initial stage of recognition, one proceeds to the next inspiration.

Path 2: The "Illuminating Intelligence"

Before going any further, let us recall the initial condition that ought to be in place before one triggers the next intelligence. One initiates a process that has been properly determined intellectually, emotionally, instinctively, and practically, and one recognises where exactly one wishes to exercise this intelligence. Thus, the process now enters the next phase: "activation."

In this phase, one is mentally engaged in evaluating what direction the activation may go in. One is involved in a practical consideration of whether things will be more or less repeated, varied, or completely changed. Emotionally, one is receptive to the distribution of these elements and sharing them with others. Instinctively, one is able to sense what direction matters will henceforth proceed. From the foundation of the initial phase of inspiration, the "Illuminating Intelligence" begins to function. To know where and with whom one wants to work is only a first step. Previously, one was dependent on ambitious activation and the domination of one centre only. Now, through familiarity with this phase, one learns how best to evaluate things and bring them into activity. At the same time, reality will reveal that not all persons involved in an enterprise will be equally ready to participate. From this path onwards, we will always have to deal with three types of persons.

The Three Common Types of Attitude One Will Face in Each Path

Within each new process initiated and spontaneously involving people within its connecting environment, one will encounter there three types of individual: the first may be called the *dependent* types; the second, those who *do not want to finish* the process; and, the third, the *independent* types.

The first type of individual is the one who strives to prove the validity of his or her own early ideas and foundations. These types are always vulnerable (through the exposure of these foundations). It makes them obliged to remain dependent upon a given learning state.

The second type of individual will at a certain moment (or from the very beginning) try to delay the process of further development because they feel that they are not really capable. This kind of individuals always finds an excuse to stop the process and attempt to stop it in such a way that their ignorance will not be noticed. It may happen that this type will begin acting from a sense of power and by this means will try to delay the process and maintain the facade of being in complete self-control. These delaying types will attempt to keep silent any dissenting voices and take every opportunity to seize control over situations by assuming a position of leadership and thus avoiding participation in any real learning process.

On the other hand, the individual who has truly and honestly undergone all processes in a complete way—which is what this stage is really about—will in the end be much more "noticeable" than the previous type of person with their façade and contrived forms of control. Nevertheless, it remains startling for the people of authenticity whose foundation is based upon a depth of enterprise to see positions of "power" filled by such fraudulent façades. One who governs processes from *within* is never noticeable by an outward silence but by a full enthusiasm and inspiration.

Such a person's appearance is more like that of someone expressing a real and lived maturity, which maintains a record of the necessary intelligence, which profoundly and properly explains and articulates the ideas behind it. This is the case because there has been added an inner reality and control that manifests itself into "excitement" during a period of propagation.

It is from such a phase of inspired self-control that this new intelligence is able to emerge. After "the first sparkle" of the previous phase, this newly discovered energy or inspiration now expresses itself through an innovative spontaneity sometimes called by Kabbalists "the second brilliance." This state reveals that something not just is managed and held together well but can also be maintained by providing new life, new confrontations, new challenges, new orientations, etc.—in short, everything that the hollow power ruler never wants to risk for fear that his or her ignorance might be exposed.

This "hollow man" would rather opt for a preservation of values that he can grasp hold of and be sure of. This condition makes all the rest impossible for him.

Only the third type of person, who has previously approached the experiences and has been touched by them, has no fear of enlarging and making complete the existing unit since a greater sense of it will be added during the creation of new initiatives. Even though some people in the group may not want to confront such propagations, nevertheless they will all (at some stage) have to deal with the results of the activity initiated by the others. The experience enfolded by the "initiator" comes forth from the experience of the 2s of each of the suits of the Minor Arcana. This experience tells us this combination of facts: a person who commits himself to these new activities is convincing in his actions because it is clear he has already been occupied with them before and has already found a supportive application in the past (2 of Pentacles). These results have indeed already ventured some favourable workout (as may be seen in the 2 of Wands) and have already involved people who have shared its efficacy (the 2 of Hearts) and with that one has also achieved some satisfaction through its reasoning process (2 of Swords). The same understandings that came from this reasoning can still be useful in the background to deal with things similarly in another application somewhere else.

Because of the conversion of the 2s into *action,* such persons continue to persevere in their enthusiasm towards others. For the public who observe or listen to such a person, it is like observing a light so luminescent that one cannot help but become inspired by it.

Path 3: The "Holy Making Intelligence"

Following the activation of full commitment, it is necessary to take care that each commitment lives its own life and finds its appropriate place. It is preferable to distinguish a full commitment to truth and openness in a protected space in which such commitment will be able to develop freely.

What now takes place in the third phase of the four types of sensory experience constitutes a combination that forms a new joint foundation for an orientation. Rationally, one has found clear direction at this stage since the path selected here only allows for and makes possible one direction for further expansion. In practical terms, this means simply that, henceforth, "there is work to be done." Emotionally, one focuses entirely on the results of this work, which consumes all one's attention. Instinctively, one senses the need to persistently address the continuity of this initiative.

With the establishment of this base, an additional intelligence is made possible, which will provide further inspiration. Through the previous path—the "Illuminating Intelligence"—an inspiration emerged that provided a kind of "knowing" how *this* had to be like *that.* From this inspiration, one was able to draw lasting results. In this next path (also called the "Sanctifying Intelligence"), these illuminations are now regarded as being "sacred." Nothing is any longer allowed to interfere with this work or permitted to distract one from completing it.

Hence, these illuminations now require a protected environment. What we have here are the truly effective elements of attention, which now need extra concentration within the protective environment. This "selective attention," which is found to be valuable or "sacred," must proceed to enlighten the whole.

At this stage, the enthusiasm obtained in the moment of taking the initiative needs to find a place to go to. Obviously, at this juncture, there will arise certain preferences. According to the 3 of Wands, one now has enough maturity to realise one's whereabouts in the process and how a complementation could improve things. This means *confinement* in a place or in a working material. The mind can no longer use its complete creative capacity. However, a limited work frame will prove most useful. Whenever the four centres of experience are confronted with such forms of awareness, it matters not what the limited selection available is for since it is certain that it will lead to the right choices because one is in communication or communion with the "voice of the heart." The restriction of the selected working material is therefore limited to those things that will allow the voice of the heart to come into its own and make the right choices. The realisation that the confirmed choice stands for a limited place in the whole pushes one to work harder on it to give it more space. One therefore "sacrifices oneself" to that *place* to become. The "sacrifice" offered to the work allows the work to receive additional value and a certain reputation. The inspiration that emerges in this kind of work purges and purifies so that the work may achieve its own "brilliance." In connection with the Kabbalah, A. E. Waite referred to this energy as being "the foundation of the Ancient wisdom, which is called the Creation of Faith."[10] In this phase, there occurs the inspiration to exclaim, "I believe in it!" which provides this intelligence with a *surplus* power.

In relation to the three aforementioned types of individuals, we have, first, those who are learning to find themselves reflected in this work; second, those who seek to maintain a dominant position and who pretend that they still have everything under control in this area; and, third, those whose inspiration is so internal that it will continue to assist the whole—even if these persons are only working on a small part of the whole. For the first two types, "faith" can only fall back on a belief that is more like a demarcation of their realised skills, knowledge, and understanding. This is especially the case for those who feel powerless and have a sense that their position has become diminished. They desire a more powerful position because they think that they deserve something better since their beliefs are so earnest and their "faith" so adamant. These persons most often articulate this "faith" in terms of some standard or norm, which fails to take into account the totality of realities, needs, and desires. These demarcations of faith are just like the power example explained above in the first phase. They are empty positions lacking any inspiration or any true knowledge of how to actually improve the whole. The faith or belief of this type can only ever be a projection of the sum of their present knowledge or abilities. Essentially, the intelligence is only able to become wisdom after exercising a practical form, a result that, without the additional incentive, cannot not be obtained. In practice, this effort only emerges as "intelligence" when one succeeds in limiting one's initiative to one's own confined work context. For those who have brought through ignorance of this process, it now becomes clear that this purging or purifying work has to do with a much-needed practical effort in general. To be open to perceiving each initiative in one's limited range of practice as a learning experience is already a step in the right direction.

Path 4: The "Receiving Intelligence"

On this path, one learns to focus on the specific point where there no longer occur any conflicts, where everyone—despite unquestionable contrasts—can work together with one another. In a rational sense, one can face existing facts directly. In a practical sense, many more features become visible, and results are made possible, which are emotionally rewarding to explore further. Instinctively, many opposites will be re-integrated within a larger structure, which makes it possible to obtain practical results that benefit the whole. The inspiration that can make this happen is called the "Receiving Intelligence."

This stage no longer manifests itself like a "calling" where one "believes" in certain things. Whilst such belief helped the like-minded to find support in a group under the form of one kind of entity or

---

[10] The above reference and all references attributed to A. E. Waite and W. Westcott, which follow, are taken from Rabbi Akiba Ben Joseph's work on the Sepher Yetzirah (Het boek der Schepping en de 32 paden der wijsheid in relatie tot het Hebreeuwse alphabet en tot de symboliek van de tarot, uitgeverij W.N.Schors, Amsterdam 1979).

another, this cannot possibly be the norm for everyone or for every essence. Therefore, one must be able to take account of the consequences of what is truly being *received* rather than simply assuming the feeling of "being inspired." This is the lesson that should already have been learned from the 4 of Wands.

It has already been explained that the practical side of certain specific choices work well with the like-minded (which are to be found spontaneously). One also knows at this stage that any emotional effort automatically directs attention to some area that generates its own mode of energy. Any fact that subsequently comes forth from such an emotion thus finds its own place. No external mentality or inspiration is required to find this. Yet certain contradictions begin to develop. For this reason, rather than fall back on just one inspiration alone—such as that of a particular belief system or faith—it is much wiser to let the new and different realities that emerge be themselves.

One can only keep a hold of the reins when the connections are sufficiently loose. This means that we must lower our guard for there exist other essences or matters that have their own forms of self-organisation within them. When it dawns on us that other elements can also be practically efficient, it will be discovered that this will still be the case when they are allowed to develop further. Such new inspirations can only be generated fully when one admits the need for their activity. Now, works are no longer coming forth from just one kind of effort, from one's own formulations or one's own actions, from casual feelings or ideas, but from the coherence of all kinds of different essences that are now able to be deployed and radiate from their own centres.

According to Westcott, "The fourth path is called measuring, being coherent or receiving, because it contains all the holy powers and all spiritual values with the most exalted essences arising therefrom; they flow from one another through the power of the primal radiance." A. E. Waite calls the inspiration in this phase the "restrained or receiving intelligence because it elevates itself as a boundary to receive the manifestations of higher intelligences that are being pulsated subsequently." One may add here that it is necessary to allow all the self-developing processes with their inspirational consistency to continue to flow freely so that they eventually become a global body.

Path 5: The "Radical Intelligence"

As the previous phase develops, it will become clear that the self-organisational will still requires a new stimulus because, over time, all the small processes together result in a diminishing clarity and consistency. Rationally, one realises the need to continue and finalise what one has. Practically, it becomes clear that the material is poorly coordinated.

Emotionally, one is struck with horror by what is inappropriate. Instinctively, the latter provides additional challenges that will be taken "graciously." In truth, one has no other choice . . .

Of course, it "makes sense" that all one's deeply ingrained values now begin to appear on the surface and express themselves one by one followed in tow by all the conditioned beliefs deeply rooted in one's essence. For this reason, one must remain aware that each inspiration can lead to a form of radicalism in its urge to make things happen. In this compressed phase of restoration, the kind of exteriorisation that is likely to occur concerns an extreme form of "Radical Intelligence" that, in itself, is convinced of values that are now experienced as being *essential*. This radicalisation of values is enhanced by the fact that these values are not associated with anything personal.

In the process of any enterprise, it will be obvious when dealing with the evident contradictions that emerge that one must try as best one can to account for the additional challenges that are likely to take shape (5 of Wands). In relation to such contradictions, one announces additional tasks and challenges under the form of norms that must be met with in each component. And this even where one has a deaf ear to it or where there exists no form of affiliation at all (5 of Hearts). One will still be able to rationally impose the values that do not wish to be heard—thanks to the gifts of the 5 of Swords—which suggests that "he who fails to hear must *feel* it."

More and more it will become clear that behind each value one thinks one stands for there exist still more deeply rooted essences. This new kind of intelligence creates a distinction between the constraints of such conditioning. It also permits one to feel the difference between the two levels: on the one hand, the personal consciousness of limiting processes and, on the other hand, that of the group bound primal essence.

Here, again, we can look to the three types of individuals, each of whom will respond differently from what happens in this phase. The first type undergoes this process and makes mistakes in certain aspects and thereby realises what is not functioning properly. This type of person is the one who is able to do something, to decide on something and make discoveries (such as we see in the fictional representation of the Magician). But it is also representative of the person who still depends on the system to learn from it (not really being conscious of playing the Fool).

The second type represents the person who refuses to enter into and accept the risks of life because he or she fears they are incapable of succeeding. This person tends to construct things with more power than skill. Abuses of power and techniques of manipulation are typical of this type.

Only the third type has "lived" and passed at least once through the four centres—instinctive, emotional, mental, and practical—in each of the phases that concern the subject matter. The person who has actually walked this path can be assured that an additional energy, an additional intelligence, and a regenerative impulse will be released.

It will become apparent that the power-abusing personality is really too radical for his own (as well as for other people's) good and therefore is completely impractical. The person who must try to open up the whole still needs a form of radicalism, but necessarily this will be of a specific order that will make a distinction between personal ignorance and the more fundamental values stood for. These values, no matter how many remain after filtering, can be nothing other than those values that are made for the good of the whole. It is this kind of values that must purify the basic mentality and renew its sources of inspiration.

Path 6: The "Intelligence of Separated Appearance"

To assemble the necessary conditions, let us line up and combine the experiences of the four cards of path 6. It has been explained how a combination of lessons from each phase, operating through the four centres of experience, form a base for a continuation of inspiration. It is this that assists in interpreting the different developmental stages of the processes in which one is directly involved in as observer.

The lessons learned in this phase are as follows: rationally, one has worked out a method by means of which one can observe all the evolving changes within any given process; practically, one recognises from this what has and has not got productive value; emotionally, one enjoys everything that has yielded some kind of value during its development; and, instinctively, one is now able to sense all the results emerging from these processes. These four experiences together give a clear indication of satisfaction and emphasise perception of the actual results.

The "radical" energy of the previous phase ensures that those whose personal choices have led to their own specific kind of limitation will experience extreme pressure. Such persons had previously fretted about whether their personality could unfold any further. Additional challenges appeared to them as heavy and burdensome. Nevertheless, regardless how stubborn or underdeveloped the person, a kind of restoration point exists here that completely breaks down all forms of radicalism and provides a separate space for the personality.

This "intermediate influence" allows once more for the full flow of abilities and personal choices. The separation of what comes from the personality and what comes from the essence provides an *additional* inspiration that makes these two different worlds work together. The advantage of this "Intelligence of Separated Appearance" is not only a higher productivity but also an enrichment of every part. Its main focus is the productivity itself focusing upon the gain of profit from the situation, which will be the same for anyone regardless of the individual programme. While the previous stage focused on placing a limit on average failure, this stage will show no limits to average productivity. The next stage will again deal with what still plays in the background with the aim of engaging this for a general stimulus.

Path 7: The "Hidden Intelligence"

In path 7, one recognises (rationally) the undeniable fact that anyone can express the essence of "being different" in a manner more extensive than one had hitherto been able to grasp. One notices those specific elements that one is not able to use practically. Emotionally, it becomes clear that one has identified too much with one's central goal and with a method that could never have delivered anything of lasting value. Instinctively, there is the need for more courage, the desire to undertake additional risks so that one may learn to deal with all the unexpected factors. One notices that some entrepreneurs will still not be ready to achieve real valuable or practical results (7 of Pentacles). One must realise that to encourage the continued underdevelopment of such things would only confirm their immature state and that the people involved will only bring forward fruitless arguments to keep them this way. In such kinds of situations, one knows how much energy is required to pick out successful arguments so that something good might emerge from the situation (7 of Swords). One also realises how much courage it requires to give all the different opinions permanent free play especially in moments when the global basis is already failing to function properly (7 of Wands). One also knows also how tempting it is not to maintain an ideal formulation at a time when one's own essence has already lost control (7 of Hearts).

There is only one thing left to do: to reassess an architectural redevelopment from a source of common belief in certain basic values of the general starting points in which people are involved.

The "Hidden Intelligence" turns itself towards a hidden appointment that each person must unconsciously confront as part of his or her responsibility to the Whole. Certain intellectual values become spiritual values that can inspire the spirit, allowing confidence in the future to grow because the right arguments for it have been made. In one sense, this inspiration can save a disintegrating group mentality by generating a renewed seriousness at its foundation. This "saving mentality" as a *hidden intelligence* is produced out of the necessity of the situation. Once the fundamental common goal has become a real foundation for inspiration, the useful aspects must be reaped and the useless aspects neglected. Once all the personal engagements and places of responsibility can be renewed and this renewing energy can become convincing to the majority, a joint energy once more begins to work seriously in an inspired way via a renewed common goal that convinces people to continue.

Path 8: The "Perfect Intelligence"

Consider now the realisation that has emerged through the experience of the four 8s. It is the combination of this experience that is the basis for the intelligence required to pass through the next path. Rationally, one recognises at this stage that for the fullness of reality to find expression, different opinions are necessary. In a practical sense, not all of these opinions are at the same level of maturity. One must take this into account when considering them, paying attention to what degree an idea has or has not come to maturity. Emotionally, this involves acceptance or tolerance towards each of these stages. Instinctively, one tends to proceed more hastily over what has not yet been properly understood. The strategy in operation here notes only what is fitting before offering it all one's attention. The less attention the imperfect and the immature receive, the more time they are given to develop into something that can become mature at a future point.

People are in need of appropriate kinds of incentives. It should be clear by now that one cannot be assured of a favourable outcome by simply believing in certain values. What can work as an incentive is to make clear to all involved that their underlying principles may be modified during periods of changing circumstances. For the sake of the group, it is best to keep the immature aspects open to one's own individual learning process before projecting them into the community. The reality will be such that it can be assured that some form of adaptability to the changing reality will further perfect these aspects sooner or later.

The inspiration for this stage can be substantiated through knowledge and acceptance that there exist situations in which nothing whatsoever can be altered further (8 of Swords). In such circumstances, it is much more important to show a good example (8 of Pentacles), while one can still be assured that for those things that cannot offer this now, it is still possible to obtain further chances to develop elsewhere and to avail of better opportunities at some future time (8 of Cups). It is important to realise that one's own ideas are never sufficiently swift enough compared with the velocity with which reality alters, nor can one's ideas ever penetrate a small fraction of the real temporal possibilities (8 of Wands). Therefore, in the present situation, one needs to acknowledge and articulate clearly the interference from all the present *impossibilities* (8 of Swords).

Through the realisation of one's limited capacity to process only the most mature of elements, one is able at last to maintain a clear vision of the whole and to no longer lose oneself on the track of inferior, incomplete, or impractical elements.

Only through the realisation of these basic conditions can one master this base completely and manage to retain the "presidential attitude"—that is to say, the permanent representative of an "absolute intelligence," which draws from the source of its own certitude.

Path 9: The "Purified Intelligence"

To further guide the circumstances in which the impractical elements remain requires a certain combination of realisations. The four 9s form the basis for the work area that permits the action of the "Purified Intelligence." For the rational mind, this brings a hard lesson (9 of Swords). Here, one realises that it is more important to attend to a broader perspective on reality than the narrow focus we have hitherto selected for our own little reality. Nevertheless, the opportunity remains to harvest all the useful results (9 of Pentacles) and realise a fertility that provides emotional spirit and joy (9 of Cups). Instinctively, one manages at this juncture to acknowledge the influx of unknown factors and to sense how these remain an important stimulus for the whole. By following the strongest energy present (9 of Wands), one limits one's alienation from the element that one experiences as unfamiliar. Of course,

133

it may happen that this estranged element is alien to the whole. Nonetheless, through following the strongest current, even the estranged learns to adapt.

Learning to account for the alienated parts increases the probability that the "foreign portion" can come to accustom itself to the whole. One can then distil the advantages of these interesting kinds of processes (9 of Pentacles) so that these "pieces of the puzzle" find assimilation into the perception of reality. Henceforth, we are able to question every thinkable thought and whence it comes. To deal with reality "as a whole" becomes a welcome new task (9 of Swords). In this way, we will be better able to integrate all kinds of freedoms to continue with the reassurance that we can further harvest and enjoy the new achievements (9 of Hearts). In the long term, this use of the *purified intelligence* treats the foreign elements in a way that tries to make something from them that can become practical whilst learning through experience.

According to A. E. Waite, "Here is avoided any classification into systems and numbering," which means that valuations that classify the situation in terms of this or that conditioned perspective are here avoided. This may refer to foreign parts in the whole, or it may refer to ourselves and to our own methods of "numbering." Hence, it is best not to interpret over and over again via the same method like some fevered Cabbalists for whom just about anything could be made to fit always to just one of the ten Sephiroth. Can such operations really explain the deeper guiding essence? Can the actual evolution and requirements of the time find any real-life renewing purpose through such translations? Is it not better to lend our attention to a more immediate insight and use its intelligence that way to give true direction? The "Purified Intelligence" is free of systems-based thinking. Yet it can still rely on the direct results emerging from any sort of practical adaptation of the four centres of experience.

Path 10: The "Glorious or Resplendent Intelligence"

This is the last path through which one instinctively brings all stages of one's motives forcibly into balance to maintain a neutralised recovery process. Here, we will be able to further correct our attitude to ensure that all of our work will remain productive for the whole. In this last phase of its kind, one is, for the first time, able to use one's rational capacity in an optimal way, dealing with its full reality having placed all stages of development into some kind of neutralised position. This full rational capacity becomes available largely, thanks to the fact that one can now discern the limited range of the rational faculties in general.

One knows that the rational faculties are mainly a tool for comparing, associating, and distinguishing. The rational faculties only really begin to become practical when one learns to distinguish between what is useful and what is not. Of course, within these various kinds of results, there are various degrees of "usability." Concerning our emotional involvement in this process, the commitment of one's sensibilities only becomes complete when one is moved by something in a given direction through all its stages of development.

From an instinctive perspective, the most important lesson here is that it is best to participate in the coordination of all developments cooperatively. This permits the involvement of more structure within everything that happens. One cannot simply leave everything to run its course and adopt the attitude that everything will naturally work itself out. This sum and conclusion of all orientations forms the basis for another kind of intelligence or inspiration that emerges at this point.

In Kabbalistic circles, it is said of this principle and its intelligence that "it illuminates the fire of all lights and reflects the strength of the formal principle." In other words, it appeals to everyone who is propelled by something and stimulates the basic principles of evolution in the sense that those propelled are able to shape themselves or can take form. Moreover, it is said that it "shows a certain degree of influence radiating from the prince of faces."

By now, it should be clear that it is more important to create a liveable world than to defend certain values in relation to the world (a lesson we have learned from the 10 of Wands). From this point of view, it is important to take more care in dealing with the mobility of a society and to adjust one's own practices in relation to it. Personal reasoning is subordinated to more general solutions (a lesson understood from the 10 of Swords). One is therefore open to whatever "final shape" will get the best working results (a lesson obtained from the 10 of Pentacles). One recognises *sympathy* (the path of affinity and easy advancement) and *antipathy* (identification with difficulties and adversities), but one does not let such "preferences" get in one's way when searching for solutions. In the light of the concept of "mentality"—as one has worked to purify it within these initial ten phases—one can say that at this tenth stage, a basic mentality could be "saved" and is henceforth able to survive in all of its further developments.

The First Ten Instinctive Stages of Recovery Applied to Use in a Company

By now, it should be quite clear how useful these ten "transcendent" phases can be when applied to developing processes within an enterprise or a business. They seem to contain something like a blueprint for an employer showing how he or she may focus on their company and the employees for whom they are responsible. To be adequately prepared for the leadership of a company, one must understand what leads to all kinds of confrontation as shown in the ten phases above. As we understand it, a leader is able to keep a healthy distance from confrontational situations and is able to maintain at all times the foundations of his enterprise. The first ten stages are the foundations for the kind of sound mentality underlying any successful business undertaking or founding of a group activity.

While not all employees work for the company with the same degree of commitment, engagement, or responsibility as the manager, most people involved will have goals of their own. In each enterprise, it is important, despite the different mentalities involved in the process, that all succeed in the common goal behind the enterprise.

The ten stages of this instinctive process

- Phase *One* involves collecting like-minded participants and material and coming forth from the basic mentality that attracts these things automatically.
- After establishing the required persons and materials, Phase *Two* directs the kind of plan agreed on and the direction in which to proceed with activities. This phase is guided inspirationally, and the representative of the enterprise ought to express an inspiring enthusiasm in which he or she represents the activation process.
- Phase *Three* describes further conditions for the work. This phase is about the concrete direction and the protected work environment. It is supported by the power of belief in the project and will discover a place where its processing can be worked out.
- Phase *Four* describes the conditions in which the available work environment is defined. This needs to be a neutral starting point that allows for personal feelings of freedom as well as promoting a productive self-organising energy, which takes into consideration individual forms of approach and the style of each member involved.
- Phase *Five* restricts personal opinions by emphasising a more general common frame (i.e., the goal of the company, which should be followed at all times).
- Phase *Six* tries to find out which limited goals employees are still involved in so as to ensure a more secure workplace in which various personalities can fit.

- Phase *Seven* aims to keep an eye on the group mentality and to find a common goal that is able to inspire all participants within the company.
- Phase *Eight* reveals it is better to focus on the productive aspects of the company and to neglect all trivialities that are not useful or that lack maturity.
- Phase *Nine* pays attention to what has been neglected or what no longer works well and will provide guidelines to limit or develop it.
- Phase *Ten* uses unexpected information gained in phase nine to better adapt to a changing world with an ever-renewing base mentality.

The above is a powerful tool for a further level of grounding. One will begin to understand every aspect that steers the world one is involved in—that is to say, the very aspects of *leadership*—which will provide a renewed focus on the steering wheel (the Chariot) now pointing towards the earth. Having worked instinctively on the sound basic mentality of all people involved, one now focuses upon a further grounding, checking further what it really is and finding out which processes really steer this world.

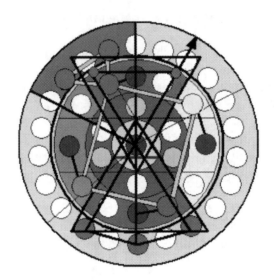

11

THE PERFECT THREE

Paths 11–13: The Three Coordinating Functions

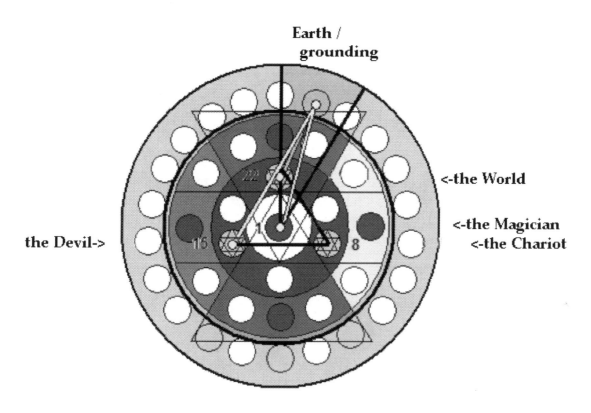

The Perfect 3: Devil-World-Magician
The three earth elements with their connecting elements (fire-water-air)

The next phase of the Third Arcana begins as a result of combining the main processes involved in navigating the paths of the Major Arcana. To do this, it connects all the "centres" of the three main areas of the twenty-two cards, which allows for a deeper *grounding* of the twenty-two (basic) situations. The Third Arcana shows the practical side as presented by the element "earth." All the centres of the Major Arcana represent a relationship with this earth element. Note that in the middle of our scheme, there is fixed only one card: the Magician. Around each centre are six cards whose *seventh* place is in the *middle*. With the Magician as card number one in the middle position, we are led to place 8, the Chariot; place 15, the Devil; and place 22, the World.

Each of these four centres represents the guiding principles for the element earth. The Devil is akin to the fire principle of the earth, the World akin to the water principle of the earth, the Magician to the air principle, and the Chariot to the earth principle, which is *neutral*.

Recall that the Chariot has already received a neutralised position in previous stages of this process.

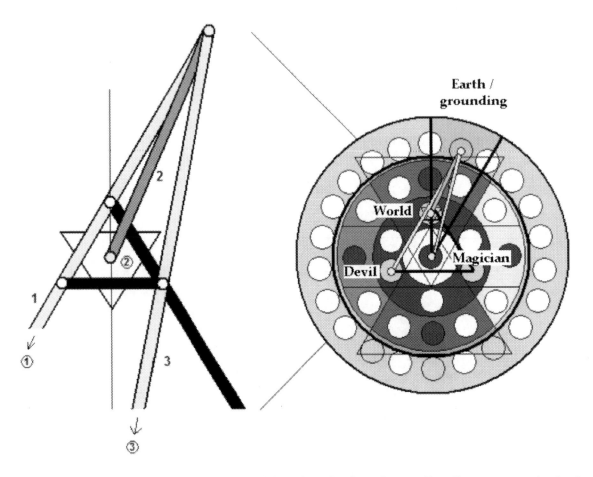

In the correct order of these guiding principles, there is, first, the Devil or fire aspect as the instinctive guiding principle, followed by the World as the fluid emotional response, and, last, the Magician as the perceptual acuity, which performs the role of a mediator. Thus, we can say that the formative processes proceed via the Devil (or the binding principle), their operative activity unfolds freely through the World, while the balance between them is maintained by the Magician.

In considering the root causes of instinctive processes on earth, one must realise that these are due to the dark aspects or shadow sides of unbalanced situations (the Devil). They are the fires of communicative creation seeking to change something in the world. The instinctive aspect related to the element fire is driven by a desire for change. Needless to say, this says nothing about "good" and "evil." We mentioned earlier that in our understanding of the tarot trumps series, the card that follows that of the Devil is the card Truth. Thus, the Devil precedes Truth and prepares the distinctions necessary for it. Hence, at this stage, things can still go in every possible direction.

The World is the second point of awareness. It is the World that steers the emotions on earth. Remember that the twenty-second card might be the card of the Fool depending on the system being followed. In the latter system, this makes the Fool the controlling factor. We have already explored this idea in an earlier chapter. The whole process of being moved can have many causes.

In earlier phases, we considered all human impulses as being "foolish" in nature in the sense that the person possessing these impulses thinks he or she needs them to become or to manifest themselves. Such persons think of themselves as "magicians." In this phase of renewal, one can learn to discern what the whole package of impulses that arise may mean in light of their first cause. In one sense, all these impulses desire to have some kind of significance in the world. On the one hand, we have the World, which steers the communications with all their actions and reactions, and, on the other hand, we have the Magician, who decides their ultimate and final form. The focal point of the Magician is *where* and *how* all contradictions coming from the World—that is to say, from the desire to become— are being controlled as a spiritual form. In this sense, the Magician works as a supervisor with responsibility for the totality of all movements.

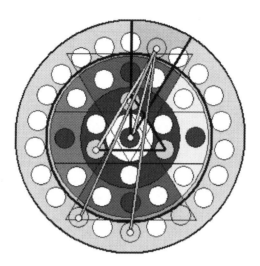

In the above diagram, I have added the *neutralised positions* of the twenty-two cards in the Third Arcana, which are represented by the three spheres in grey (again as 3 x 7). The control being exercised by the earth principle (which normally stands for the practical state) now shows the Magician in the *middle* of the different energies not only operating as a "ruler" but also operating in a dependent position in relation to events. The Magician is supported by two energies, which have become neutral in their position and which originate from the principles of the Devil and the World, who themselves have become neutral only after having been guided through the combined focus of the Magician. The new paths that are drawn from them represent the energies that provide *inspiration* and *insight* in this position. One might also say that the effects of the Devil and the World at this juncture are being healed or neutralised, while the Magician continues to maintain an active role in the process.

In Kabbalistic studies, this totality consists of three paths each with their own intelligence and appropriate names, which result from a correct understanding and guidance of these processes. They are presented by the path of "the Fiery Intelligence" (the first phase seen from the cause: the Devil), the "Intelligence of Light and Transparency" (seen from the operative action itself: the World), and "the Guiding Intelligence of the Unit" (viewed from the position of final results: the Magician).

It is extremely important to grasp the nature and position of these three cards and their causal function in influencing processes in the world of events and also to understand how they are the guiding principles for all underlying inspirations. Now, we will turn our attention to a more in-depth exploration of each of these paths.

Path 11: The "Fiery Intelligence"

He who understands the principle of the Devil or can properly take into account the position of this card (as expressed in the context above) can predict its presence. From this position, one no longer makes any distinctions between "higher" and "lower" causal impulses. In the previous phases, one has worked on integrating strange and alien impulses. Each of these impulses wanted to signify something and to fight for its own place. In the previous stage, we coordinated these impulses to integrate them in a practical way. Having progressed through the last ten stages, it should also be clear by now that the principles of evolution are the same for everyone. Now, one is ready to take into account more general archetypal conditions. The person who has the insight to recognise these general principles displays a certain dignity because he or she carries those higher and lower impulses within them.

In Kabbalistic studies of the thirty-two paths, this phase has to do with *transmutation*. This is easy to understand because the notion that things can change—sometimes to something "better" and sometimes to something "worse"—depends on the *viewpoint* and the cause and consequences attributed to things. In this phase, all impulses can be transformed into wisdom, thanks to this "Fiery Intelligence," which is concerned with human drives and desires. Here, all fiery impulses are forces amenable to use on earth.

This principle can be compared with the perspective of the clever politician who has a keen judgement and is able to disarm his adversity because he is able to gauge the general trend of mind and specific limitations of the other. He has learned that this is not based on any kind of dualistic appraisal but rather about a form of coordination that is itself much more powerful. The politician's insight into the weaknesses of his opponent gives him the power to overpower or reduce the other and prevents him from bringing anything against him. At first sight, the politician's counterarguments appear to be invincible and irrefutable. He expresses a *fiery intelligence*. He is a little devil. He has instilled within his own person the characteristics of the tarot card the Devil in such a way that a certain dignity is brought to his person bestowing upon him a certain power to rule, as well as a tactical ability to disarm opponents with the strength of his arguments. "Transmutation" in this particular sense means that everything can take on another form, and everything can take on a new order and arrangement so that much more can be done. This keen insight can suddenly bring forth fantastic proposals for accomplishments that will remain long in history as, for example, in the case of the Napoleonic laws.

Those persons who still think they need "divisional values" and are not ready for any form of integration need to find other outlets for this energy. Only what is a fixed value for all will be able to be "bundled together." This is in fact the first intelligence that makes decisions that seem to have extended over restrictive arguments. For others, it will be unclear where all these new ideas are coming from and whether they are being produced by a higher or lower aim. Perhaps both good and bad intentions will enter into the mix here. Perhaps one will not really have control over it or be able to check it. In any case, one is likely to be so results minded that the effects in the long term will be overlooked because one will be so preoccupied with the willpower one considers necessary to cause adjustments.

Path 12: The "Intelligence of the Light"

The second principle that is operational in the World is akin to water that binds itself with earth. The earth stands for everything that is viewed as "practical" and "useful" on earth. One might consider that everything that has to do with this principle attracts people towards each other, evokes desires and emotions, and always and everywhere has to do with the world itself. In fact, it is the world (or society) that controls it more than we do ourselves. This means that we realise there exists a certain sequence or order in the appearance of our impulses.

It is a fact that our instinct to survive and to change arises from our mistakes, which bind us to the earth. For this reason, the earth beckons us to be more practical because it is the place where the results of our failures are exposed. Indeed, trying to address failures is the basis of the urge to be significant in the world. The world distributes such impulses and encourages people who would like to respond to them, who see potential in them, people for whom it is worth the trouble to do something practical with them. If you know this already, then you will also know that there is no "motion" from people; rather, it has to do with their own lack of place in the world. One would like "to be a player."

The "fiery power" of the coordinating ability previously mentioned can only continue to be realised as an insight when it is fed from something that goes beyond the initiative of any personal vision or ideas. In the previous stage, finding some useful future images had been difficult because it demanded another kind of vision of things. In this subsequent phase, the mentality adapts itself to these "visions," which offer further opportunities to release the imagination into projects with which one is involved.

As an example of this, imagine what a degree of DNA manipulation might result in. Every specific piece of data is here exploding with possibilities through the imagination that is opening up to future paths. It seems as if the whole world is open before one. This intelligence is called the "Intelligence of Transparency" or the "Intelligence of Light." The fire of the first phase of coordination is here being tamed with water and now acts as a "guiding principle" to the present emotional connections, desires, and the like that are seeking a way out. It is important to see this not only as an astral desire that takes shape in the world but also as an insight and power of imagination, which is trying to find a way to become true in the world. It is like getting an insight into all these desires simultaneously and trying to find a place for them so that they can mean something upon the earth.

The previous intelligence came to understand that all instinctual impulses represent stages of formation. Now, we come to understand that guiding principles are involved and behind them the expectation of things themselves, which look for a response through the process of becoming. Each of these "separate wills" wants to be acknowledged, to be heard, to obtain emotional satisfaction. In this phase, it will also become clear that there exists no ultimate good and evil. All this so-called willing is just "fire" seeking expression. Each impulse has within it another cause. Obviously, a frustrated person will work more aggressively in this process of becoming compared with someone who has already succeeded in finding answers and channels. While the drive towards "fulfilment" is an imbalance nevertheless, the emotional process of becoming will continue to behave according to its nature. In essence, there is no difference in the *process of becoming* between the person who fails and becomes frustrated and the person who succeeds and experiences a good mood. What makes this intelligence *transparent* and inspiring is due to our diligent care for what emerges.

Path 13: The "Guiding Intelligence of Unity"

Ordinarily, a person tends to fall back upon the ego because he or she believes that it is the one true centre that keeps all actions and processes under control. This is also the chief reason why man is apt to think of himself as a "magician," even though in actuality he is entirely dependent on situations. For the most part, his "manipulations" only distance him from what is actually necessary, whilst his real development is often painfully slow or hopelessly delayed. Yet he is still a Magician in the light of the creative process of becoming itself. He is, or can be, the manipulator, the delayer, or the entrepreneur. He remains a responsible ruler of impulses and decisions as to whether to take the initiative. What he does *not* decide is the presence of impulses emerging from the world and the intense emotionality that he feels welling up from this world. Such impulses or intensities are simply there. This is so because there are imperfections in the world and all things are searching to find resolution and to attain to the sense of wholeness. What a man does have under control is the mental form, which he attributes to things. Thus, he is the Magician in his capacity to alter and manipulate his own representations of the world, but he has no control over the presence of intensities existing within circumstances and events— not even when he does what he "must do." In this respect, the personal control of the ego is very limited. It has responsibility over a mental form, which must be worked upon in the process of becoming before there can be any possible improvement of the form that is eventually received by the world at large.

The Magician learns to become more efficient in the world when he learns to express Truth better and more clearly and in a way that the imbalances inherent in the impulses of the world and in the intensities of other people's emotional responses may themselves be improved. The Magician remains the foundation of the "I want" (or self-will), of the development of the personality and the creation of a personal world through choice. As such, the Magician is the focal point of counter-reactions and can only become a respected force when he is clearly articulating his own truth.

Just as with the positions of the Devil and the World, there does not exist at this juncture a classification of good and evil, because this kind of classification is irrelevant. This is not to say that people are failing to handle effectively the creative process of becoming or taking adequate responsibility for themselves. At this stage, one makes no distinction any more between a person who is inspired by a higher necessity and one who comes forth from a base of frustration. Any person who commences his becoming mentally is controlled by a common principle of continuous creation. In this sense, the principle of "continuous creation" refers to a practice that must be constructed mentally before being considered as possessing any value. By "mental," we mean here *psychologically sane*: courageous, responsible, a serious conduct of the will in man.

All of the above three phases or coordinating functions can be considered in terms of an individual and their personal handling of events. Where Paths 1–10 were concerned with grounding the base *mentality*, Paths 11–13 are concerned with grounding the *form of a personal coordination* of processes.

According to A. E. Waite, this new accompanying principle is sometimes called the "Guiding Intelligence" because it provides a kind of gravity and guidance that is always accompanied by a degree of responsibility. One can understand this phase and its inspiration better when we meditate on the meaning of the card the Magician when applied in various combinations.

The Next Three Instinctive Grounds of Recovery When Applied to Use in a Company

All of the above three phases or coordinating functions can be considered in terms of an individual and their personal handling of events or in terms of a leader or head of an organisation and the handling of the practical affairs of a business. Where Paths 1–10 were concerned with grounding the *mentality* with which a company and its members were assembled, Paths 11-13 are concerned with grounding the *form of a personal coordination* aimed at coordinating processes with which the company can be steered further. In terms of a business or company,

- in stage 11, the requirement is to coordinate without distinction or preferences. In this way, one learns to know one's opponent's limits while one displays none of one's own. All impulses used for change will be found to be useful.
- in stage 12, if you set yourself to imagining future projects, do so without limits. Thus, you will cross the boundaries of planning and expectation. All efforts in this direction will prove to be useful.
- in stage 13, know that the only real aspect of self-control is mental, and every improvement in articulation, no matter how personally engaged, is useful. It is thanks to such articulations that things can become real.

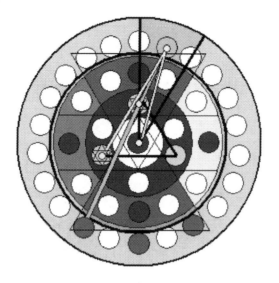

The transition towards the next series

12

THE HOLY AND CONFLICTING SEVEN

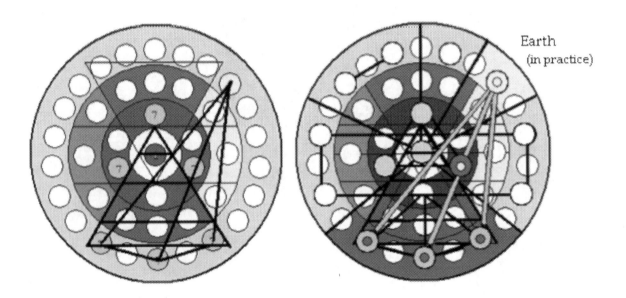

Earth
(in practice)

In the previous three phases, a transition was in operation that provided the instinctive aspects with some additional grounding. Now, in the next developmental block of the Third Arcana, the earth element will receive some further grounding. If we look at the diagrams above, we will notice that the one on the top left indicates how we might begin to achieve an increased integration of all twenty-two stages of the Major Arcana. In the other diagram (top right), it becomes clear how the last "doubled connection" with the element earth—that is to say, with the Carriage (or control)—previously did not have an opportunity to make an active connection. In the stage that follows, it will now get the opportunity to integrate its active processes.

Recall that the Major Arcana initially showed us a helpless man subject to the *automatism of the principal functions*, and the Minor Arcana revealed to us a man *learning through experience* the nature of the four centres and their intimate relationship to the four elements. The initial stages of the Third Arcana have made it clear that man is working towards *conscious integration* (Paths 1–10) and a *coordinated becoming* (Paths 11–13). It is now time to put into perspective our own role in the whole event.

The next process of awareness therefore consists of seven phases. As mentioned earlier, the twenty-two cards consist of 3 x 7 phases (+ 1 joint centre). People appear to experience the "divided equilibrium" most easily through a sevenfold development. The circulating phases perform a mobile balance between the elements, orchestrating relationships between different worlds, between different experiential bodies at different levels, correlating everything. A person who fails to recognise something in one area will still have the chance to see it or to learn from it or to make something better as a whole on another plane. All of this is the significance to us of "the world of 7."

The twenty-two become the "real" world in which the proportionate world of 7 is presented. Together, they enable the complete physical reality of all phase-oriented relationships. The following seven paths of the Third Arcana correspond to a learning process that embeds these kind of proportional relationships.

Path 14: The "Luminous Intelligence"

The tarot card associated with path 14 is the Sun. Waite calls this stage the "Illuminating Intelligence" and says of it, "It is the founder of the Arcana." As already mentioned, the hidden meaning of the number 22 is 3 x 7 (+ 1 centre). Thus, every 7 appears as two interlocking triangles each with one centre. There exists a rhythm within the process of becoming that is much more than a numerological order cut to fit a single system. This rhythm, within which one finds an increasing number of relationships, is practical because through it things find a balance of opposites and complements. The nature of this rhythm is the reason why certain patterns in the cosmos, geometrical and otherwise, are followed to one degree or another.

This particular path with its central focus on the Sun is referred to in Kabbalistic studies as the path of "Wisdom and Foolishness." In the previous three phases, it did not seem to matter whether a design was good or bad because all was a form of becoming. From here on, however, such distinctions are going to matter. Unlike the Magician, who "becomes" simply because he cannot help from doing so, the Sun is a centre whose responsibility is more than just a choice. The "choice" of the Sun is not like that of the Magician or, for that matter, like that of the Fool. In the path of the Sun, the reality of its present elements has become most true, real, and inevitable. Now, the choice of what to do with those elements is made for the first time. The scales of the elements are no longer subject to action and reaction as they were in the previous card. Here, all "fitting relationships" are already established. Here, the question is, *What path do you choose to pursue?* Will you take the path of the Fool or the path to the attainment of Wisdom? And what are you yourself through this coordination: Fool or Sage? It is only truly now that one recognises one's own share in the processes.

A peculiar characteristic of the Sun is that *in itself* it always shines, but on earth its luminescence depends on *certain phases*. In itself, the Sun is always what it is. It is constant. Yet it is only fully significant to the human observer on earth when it shows its light in phases. It appears to shine exactly when it should but hides itself when the earth requires rest and peace. To live the meaning of the card the Sun is not, as one might think, akin to living the meaning of Leo, who always desires to be at the centre of things. "To be the Sun in all circumstances" requires much more flexibility than this. Unlike the Leo principle, it requires a greater degree of *mobility* in fixed positions. The sign Leo might correspond to a sun-oriented character, but this refers only to a personality type. In this case, the Sun is seen from the perspective of a whole group of people. But the Sun itself may be considered as adapting to our world, not by changing itself but by signifying something different in different places in our world. It is the conditions of the earth itself that determine what is admissible and what is not. Thus, from one perspective, Wisdom may be thought of not so much as an aim but as a form of adaptation. In the "Zen Moment," which is put to the test in Zen Buddhism, there are no fixed answers to the questions being stated. Each unique moment and individual circumstance requires a different adjustment. Whoever understands this principle "possesses" Zen wisdom. The latter is a good example of the man who can adapt to the moment. Something of this Zen principle shines through here. In fact, only by shining through the situation can one be a shining example.

The intelligence that is learned at this juncture is called the "Luminous Intelligence" because it can radiate the shining example and express the intelligence of the mobility of the world itself. It is always perfectly placed (like the shining example), which may, depending on the occasion, be either wise or completely foolish. For those of you for whom the idea of the mobile Sun is strange, let us repeat that the balance that is created here and focused on the Sun is formed from the viewpoint of the earth— that is to say, from the place where all human inhabitants presently reside. The major shift that has taken place at this point is similar to the kind of collective shift that took place around the seventeenth century and inaugurated the period of the "Enlightenment." Instead of the personality now being at the centre of everything, a radical shift in perspective occurs that identifies the Sun as the centre of our system.[11]

Path 14 is very much about adapting to the *Now Moment* by realising what processes really steer the visible world. It is also about understanding what is needed at each point in time. By receiving light and attention and by being surrounded by impulses to become or not become, one is able to adapt well. The next stage will show its opposite or dark aspect. What if something ought not see the light of day? What if something ought to be neglected? Might things develop better through other things not receiving any attention? What needs the light of day should be given attention. Other things should not—in the same way that one's position and opinion is not always important when it has not developed from the impulse of the moment.

Path 15: The "Constituent intelligence"

When confronted with the question of accepting or refusing higher positions, of moving towards or away from glory and fame at the moment when it would only provide a pyrrhic victory, it is often asked whether position, power, and money are not more important than the idea of dying impoverished, but with honour. In describing this path, A. E. Waite refers to a passage from Job and to the fact that creation is formed in darkness. This phase encourages one to think about one's position during its creation and offers a different perspective on the usefulness of having certain positions at the moment when one is attempting to change something. As in the previous phase, this moment requires relativisation with regard to certain concepts. In the previous phase, the "moment" was based on Wisdom versus Foolishness. In this phase, the concepts concerned are those of Wealth versus Poverty. Here, one must learn to reconcile their necessity and true meaning.

A rich man may be considered poor in spirit or a poor man rich in spirit. Everything depends on the perspective adopted. At a given moment, the interior condition or state of the so-called wealthy man may actually be rather impoverished, and the situation of the so-called poor man rich (or vice versa). Therein lies our answer: if a situation impoverishes one from within, no amount of outer richness can save one from disaster. On the other hand, when a situation really enriches one from within, an outer amelioration is sure to follow. The intelligence necessary in this arena is called the "Constituent Intelligence" because it adapts itself to what is best for the whole set of circumstances regardless of what those circumstances happen to be. Thanks to this intelligence, the question will no longer amount to a choice between "Wealth" and "Poverty."

Behind this dilemma lies a different steering mechanism. In any given circumstance, "wealth" may be best considered from the point of view of whether something can work to "enrich" the environment. Sometimes, one thing or another may or may not work to enrich the circumstances (as viewed from the perspective of the earth). This important idea has little to do with individuals and their personal desires and more to do with circumstances that ought to be provided for through their own necessities. Once more, this new "focus" concerns the *essence* that works to enrich the world and the earth. The

---

[11] In volume 2 of *The Fool's Tarot*, it will be shown what these annual phase shifts mean to us and how we can understand them by comparing them with the phases of the Major Arcana. It will also be revealed how we can come to understand the meaning of each of the cycles of the traditional seven planets and the twelve constellations by comparing this with the movement and position of the Sun on earth during a full year's cycle.

outer forms of these results are only of relative importance. The emphasis here remains on balancing experience—that is to say, on showing which choices need to be made and which do not. Thus, the only form of enrichment that will not cause imbalance in the world comes forth from an inner preparation (outside of any circumstances), which evaluates what is necessary to *restore harmony* to the environment.

Path 16: The "Eternal Intelligence"

In this stage, we are led to the question of whether it is a good thing to create (at any time). The card that answers this question emerges from the results of the Chariot or the Carriage, which is the "steering mechanism" already mentioned in the previous series concerned with the coordinating principles. It is the centre that forms the basis for the *power to neutralise* everything that happens on earth.

Recall that almost everything automatically called into life by man is a kind of form that is initially out of balance with nature. Such forms seek to "become" because they are imperfect. All that becomes requires adjustment. What will transpire in the end are the things that possess the power to neutralise imbalances not by stopping them from becoming but by providing them with structures that permit them to become fruitful or render them extinct by destroying them, so that they can no longer continue in an impractical form. The best results emerge from those things that help the earth survive in a more viable way. The contradiction to be overcome here concerns the concepts of "Fertility" versus "Destruction." According to Waite, this path is also called "the victorious and eternal intelligence" as well as "the delight of the glory, the paradise of pleasure prepared for the righteous."

There are lots of values established and worked out within societies that try to ensure that everything that is created finds a means of being channelled. This is to ensure that the useless elements remain unusable and the useful elements continue to be conducive to function. For an understanding of how this happens, it is best to examine again the meaning of the card the Chariot (or the victory wagon) as it adapts itself to all kinds of circumstances. The Chariot indicates that even when one possesses a so-called great personality and can remain firmly on course in such a way that regardless of circumstances one never fails to deny oneself and seems to bring forth something good or at least something productive, one need not take advantage of this fact through an insatiable urge to overcome always and everywhere.

In practice, one learns that the principles of Victory/Defeat that concerns one here do not have the same meaning for others (for their vision or circumstance). It is often important and more effective to win only when the victory means profit for all. If one maintains an image of oneself as the "victor" at all times, this may have a devastating effect on the expected results. Learning to know when and where to be humble and where and when to be spontaneous without feeling the need to force anything means learning this "Eternal Intelligence." With this intelligence, one is able to retain, in all circumstances, an apparent naivety, which is, in reality, a conscious openness that reflects a paradisiacal state of innocence. This explains why this path is also called the "Delight of Glory" or "the paradise of pleasure, prepared for the righteous." This intelligence creates the path of fertility and destruction.

This means that to lead the situation effectively, it is necessary to allow some things to come to fruition while accepting that other things must be aborted or discontinued. In this way alone can such wisdom survive and not become a form of displaced arrogance. The aspects of "Eternal" intelligence, which Waite refers to, might also suggest we keep in mind what continues to persist or survive. This is not necessarily about retaining certain values but rather concerns the continuation of values, which remain workable and productive whilst expressing the separation characterising the concepts of "Fertility" versus "Destruction."

The lesson we draw from this stage is that the needs of the moment will decide what is or is not useful for a further evolution (in terms of viability for all). If one posits a norm through misjudgement, it will be broken down. The only place where one remains in control is in a *neutral place* without emotional disturbance and the distraction of limiting thoughts—a place where one remains wholly attentive to the needs of each moment.

Path 17: The "Sensible Decision Intelligence"

In the previous phase, one may have allowed certain capacities and values to survive in a modest role. In this next phase, a further step is necessary that surrenders representation of any kind of capacity and values so as to share *anonymity* with present movements. It is here that one learns the "Sensible Decision Intelligence." Sometimes, "not being there" is important to allow a situation to return to a basic fundamental balance. A person who understands the meaning of the tarot card Death in every possible circumstance understands that the *essence* of many situations is very often completely outside his own knowledge parameters and that the essence that remains and will be useful in the long term can only manifest itself in the *pure surplus* residue of the completed situation. It is said of this stage that allowing to such awareness, "it becomes the basis for excellence in the state of higher things." In other words, let the right foundation manifest itself after the acceptance because such essence is not to be found in oneself. It is also said "it makes the pious agree to persevere and makes them ready to receive the Holy Spirit." This means that only the one who can *release himself completely* is able to receive the essence of all that is necessary.

This path is also called the "Path of Life or Death." One can look to situations in the hope of learning to "live" only there where life *is*. Sometimes, this means keeping a distance from life and recognising that life might have a place "somewhere else." If one fails to recognise this, one risks "being killed." Thus, instead of making a "life or death" decision, this intelligence brings a different insight because one is able to look directly at and beyond the situation.

Some creative processes cannot be accomplished until we develop a certain distance from conventional concepts. Only when that distance has become real can the whole situation continue to evolve. A known process—which is dead in the here and now—can no longer be forced any further. The reality here is that two processes have come together that do not belong together. Each process has its own rhythm and its own phases. What vitalises one process and not another shows that there must be some form of separate evolution taking place that permits a future for the former. Some evolutionary changes must be left to other influences or milieus of concern. And this is also the wise decision that is expected of *you*. Leave it to someone else. Let it go. Leave well alone and learn your lessons from it. Keep your distance at all times from things that are not your business. This way, each separate evolution can take its own proper course.

Path 18: The "Radiating Intelligence"

It is imperative that more and more people begin to realise to what degree their own personal efforts are useful in constructing something greater. It is only in certain specific "places" that the effect of one's personal influence, in combination with the accumulation of a certain life wisdom, can really be decisive in all circumstances and be felt as truly "appropriate" for anyone who encounters it. When a person has properly inhabited this "righteousness of an appealing place," he has learned the lesson of the tarot card we call the High Priest in each circumstance.

Knowing where best to enhance one's "practice" further and where best not to continue any further bestows a certain dignity on the beholder of such wisdom and results in the respect of all. With this insight, one deals with one's own position and keeps an eye on one's own territory at all times. In fact, this is exactly the place where this kind of insight is received. The conscious limitation of one's own centre is engaged with a responsibility that generates extra power to change things in a way that everyone will benefit from.

Thus, such a person knows how to create the conditions for this sort of change and how to increase the flow of good (or useful) things in the direction of his or her fellows. People realise that this kind of a person respects everyone's boundaries as well as their own. Certain essential truths will be revealed to such a person, and through them the development of potentialities for an entire population of people is made possible in a context where the right kind of wheel puts the right kind of gears in motion (automatically). The challenge to act in terms of the right incentive, in the right place, at the right time becomes a pearl of wisdom when one knows that one's own function is both a guiding and responsible one.

The intelligence to be used in this situation is called the "Radiating Intelligence." Waite says of this path, "from here are drawn forth the Arcana and the hidden meanings which rest in the shade of it." The contradictions that this detached intelligence is able to overcome have to do with "Domination" versus "Slavery." *Where do we have this state of affairs where someone feels himself a slave to a system? At what point does someone feel dominated by someone else's values? At what point does someone make it so?* These are questions one will no longer be concerned with when one is able to handle this intelligence that now focuses on the recognition of a responsible force within one's own distinct world. Where the previous path exposed a sense of "separateness" from the distinct working processes, here the strength of individual processes is promoted and recognised. In fact, one no longer pays any attention to whether one's values come over well to others. One knows that when one's values are well defined within themselves, they will be a good example to those who need them.

The lesson of this stage is that it is best not to go around criticising and pointing out all that is "wrong" in the narrow and imprisoned worlds that one recognises. Instead, one uses such information to understand one's own specific world of ideas and values and to restore what is missing in one's own little world. This will be inspiring to the extent that one is able to solve things by and for oneself.

Path 19: The "Intelligence of the Secret of Spiritual Activities"

From this point onwards, one will begin to notice the manner in which significant spontaneous interactions "become" in the moment. Once sufficient respect is shown for the personal developmental processes and the individual leadership of others numerous possibilities will emerge for something spontaneous to occur. For the first time, a real interaction of gears and wheels begin to interconnect.

Speaking of this intelligence, Waite says, "It is the secret of all spiritual activity. The fullness which it reaches comes from the highest blessing and glory." The contradiction that is overcome through this new mode of intelligence concerns the concepts of "Peace" and "Misfortune." The risk attending the possibility of contradiction between "Peace" and "Misfortune" can be here avoided so that the number of instinctive and emotional exchanges involved can be lessened.

Here, one must ask, What perspective has one mapped out for oneself, and how does this perspective fit in with others? It is only when a *joint perspective* becomes the inspiration that the ideas of all can be expressed safely. As soon as one understands how this situation provides perspective on the things that crosses one's path, one understands to what extent coincidences possess synchronicity, and thus one can feel assured one can derive peace and solace therefrom. From that moment of realisation, one confronts the unknown face to face, desiring to make nothing else from it than that the whole fit inevitability within it.

The situation of the previous phase ("Slave" versus "Domination") had been overcome through the discovery of one's "shielded place" and the possibilities of that place. We came to understand that this is the only working area that creates opportunities and becomes much more than simply one's personal fate. Indeed, all fated consequences in an experienced history need not be insurmountable but can possess ordinary factuality as well as offering new starting points. Before this can happen, however, one's personal point of departure with all its attendant shortcomings must be fully acceptable to one. One must learn to make peace with *all*. Every shortcoming and "misfortune" is rooted in one's own rhythm, whilst also the whole itself has a rhythm of its own. People who have received a "working area" within the whole have a working rhythm that will suit their own pace when they fully take up their responsibility and make peace with the whole, with themselves and their imperfections. In this way, they may come to "mean" something within the two joint rhythms. This is no longer a question of maintaining a critical stance in relation to the different nature of these rhythms because it has become clear that each of these rhythms must fit one's own responsibilities. When one finally gets "into rhythm," it means learning to handle these responsibilities. Here, in this place, are two different working rhythms that together constitute the "spiritual potency" of a group activity. What a person contributes to this area—through expressing a willingness to cooperate with the whole—influences this joint rhythm.

Through the meaning of the tarot card the Star, one ought to adapt this idea to any circumstance and to draw inspiration from the coordinating intelligence to transcend the various dilemmas raised by it. The Star stands for the *rhythms of destinies*, and upon discovering these rhythms, one begins to live and adapt as best one can to the rhythm of these discoveries. The Star is also the rhythm of anticipation. Everything that flows through the mind, impulsively, emotionally, and so on, determines the direction(s) one takes. If one makes the choice to release something at the "crossing point" of a situation, this may serve to progress the entire rhythmical pulsation and thereby determine the rest of the rhythms. A person who understands this and can find peace with it has a budding point for additional insights. The misfortune, which hitherto was connected to a previous focus on his specific personal rhythm, will now cease to be. From that moment, new ideas will be able to emerge that will break the chains of fate.

A few pointers may be in order at this moment on how best to meet unfortunate circumstances. First of all, it is necessary to recognise the totality of the various rhythmical interactions that will decide in a more or less fluent way the full development of all one's potential abilities. Before adding one's own proportion, one had to take one's destiny into one's own hands by being able to stand completely outside these rhythms and imagine a new destiny by making something constructive out all of its previous elements.

It should be clear by now that simply adopting a positive or hopeful attitude alone will not bring any positive results. One is only able to alter misfortune when one accepts and realises that something is not assisting the rhythm of life itself because of flaws and imperfections. This is something that cannot be solved through "good initiative." The permanent resistances can be considered a learning process for a group-based interactive spiritual activity. At this stage, the existence of any previous struggle no longer matters because an independent process of articulation and searching for a path in an interactive environment has already begun. The lesson of this stage is to realise that imperfections in oneself and in the world have comparable rhythms when combined and show the same destiny in their becoming.

Once one discovers the common solutions that will integrate these things into the rhythm of life, a larger context emerges that works as an inspiration for everyone involved in the same task.

Path 20: The "Intelligence of the Will"

Whoever tries to restore order to an unhappy fate needs a certain degree of courage because things by themselves do not immediately come into a favourable rhythm. For most people, restoration will be a question of learning to adapt to the emergence of "other kinds of energy." These "other kinds of energy" come into the foreground because they are the values that are important *now*.

This was not properly understood before because one had not integrated these energies or did not know them or had never wished to integrate them. At some point, it will be impossible to prevent surrender to these energies. For this reason, it is better to learn to accept them and come to an understanding of what these energies are (and also what the term "inadequate" really means).

The Hanged Man suspended from the Tree of Life refers to ancient initiations. The "hanged one" learns to surrender, to give up all personal struggle. For too long, the struggle against unseen resistances and limitations has continued unabated until at last one learns to sense the energy of the Tree (or larger structure) to which one is attached. The pulsing energy within the Tree itself (which one can feel after being attached to a tree for three days) is the true rhythm or movement of nature and the world. Those who have, in one way or another, felt "condemned" at first by this rhythm have not taken into account the standards necessary to maintain the movement properly in keeping with all the phases necessary for their evolution. While the "condemned" may feel themselves victims of the movement, it is rather they themselves who, through denial, have caused these woes through failure to deal with events. The current of energy that turns back upon such persons and must now be endured is proportionate to their own inadequacies, ignorance, and imperfection.

However, by retaining one's dignity during this phase of the process—that is to say, undergoing the unknown factors and experiencing the fate of the Hanged Man in all circumstances—one learns to produce a renewed essence, which can once again become useful and practical. The contradiction to be overcome at this juncture has to do with "Grace" versus "Ugliness." The person who has not managed to integrate the more powerful energy first always has an aversion to it. Such a person finds it "ugly." The dominant energy regards itself as the dignified energy opposed to the non-integrated and ugly "pimple" on the face of the whole. Both energies follow these predictable roles, which are relatively interchangeable depending on position.

This is not about what position or viewpoint is the correct one. What inspires here and is necessary is the adoption of a "good will" to adapt energies without judgement or condemnation. Of course, circumstances will impose constraints such that the least integrated is obliged to integrate the most novel. This can feel like a punishment or resistance, yet the goal behind it is general recovery. Waite explains, "It prepares all created beings, each individually, for the detection of the existence of the original glory." The will is also the willingness to perceive "grace" and to view it as an opportunity that can be granted to the situation so that its existence is released and its possibilities experienced.

One can only atone for something through a restored "will" as soon as that will emerges from one's own strength and is no longer brought forth from any other outside force or from a "will from beyond." Everything one is able to accomplish with this new kind of situation is put into perspective by keeping oneself in the background (when necessary) and by recognising where productivity can occur by letting the energy flow to where it is needed. Where such energy cannot bring anything productive, it is best to maintain a distance from it.

By restoring a "willingness" to integrate with "the other," one increases one's focus. The circle of one's focus becomes larger and begins to take on an elliptical shape. Originally, the Kabbalists used the idea of the ellipse as a widened circle with two foci instead of one. We come to this as a result of the previous three coordinating functions. The change of form from circle to ellipse can be compared to the orientation of man's position inside a variety of other influences. Thus, at one time, the earth was presented within a solar system in which the seven main planets were symbolically considered as the main influences determining human destiny. The position of the Sun at the centre remained comparable to an *individualised principle* acting in the role of "leader." Within the concept of the ellipse, which is an extension of the previous circular solar system—which opposes the earlier idea of Earth as the centre—the second focal point of the ellipse may include several extra focuses.

The association of this notion of the ellipse was simply a case of not only drawing comparisons between inner and outer worlds but also the positing of a concept of an outer and inner sun. In this respect, we may ask, What exactly is meant by the term "spiritual sun" understood as a second kind of focal point? From a physical perspective, the answer may be that this second focus, along with all of its associations, remains related to the fact that the sun of our system is itself orbiting around another centre located near the star Sirius. The reason why the movements of the planets are elliptical has to do with the fact that their gyrations depend on another secondary motion. A similar movement can be discovered in all rhythmic processes that receive such a secondary "pull." This means that in experiencing the reality of this or that movement, we must always take into account another kind of movement. It is this attitude of taking into account secondary adjustments within a cycle whose ongoing processes are not directly visible from the perspective of one person or one vision alone that constitutes the profound meaning of the Arcanum the Hanged Man. One might say that the Hanged Man depends on more rhythms than any single vision could encompass. Thus, without a true willingness to examine real intersections and investigate the problems pertaining to various rhythms, each will continue to preserve something "retarded" or "inappropriate." If, however, one willingly examines things from the perspective of a *joint focus*, a renewal and recovery of certain essences is made possible.

Although we can think of Earth as representative of man in the midst of other forces, it is the Sun that obviously possesses the greatest and most direct influence upon man. We know that both the Sun and the other planets in our solar system all have "another centre" located in the centre of our galaxy and that this "point" itself also revolves around the "Central Sun." Further focal points will therefore indicate greater or more extensive evolutionary movements whose rhythmic effects (for now at least) it would be almost impossible to apprehend within the limitations of our own temporal existence. Hence, it is not necessary to concern ourselves with these various foci. If we examine which influences have very definite determining affects upon our own lives, we need look no further than the cycles of the Sun and the Moon along with the rhythmic cycles of their neighbours: Mercury, Venus, Mars, Jupiter, and Saturn. These seven paths or "pendular movements" all reveal the human being's integration into a larger context.

Taken as a whole, this representation indicates man's position within a process of interactive counter-oscillations and complementary principles. Regarding these seven direct influences, one will have noticed that the orbiting influences are not only moving towards one centre that concerns them but also, in an elliptical fashion, moving towards a feedback centre with which the whole cycle of events circle from one "edge" to the next.[12]

---

[12] When we investigated the inhibited processes of recovery in the Major Arcana in a previous chapter, it was briefly explained how a learning process that encourages, provokes, and works with a student (pupil or initiate) is needed to shape

We have spoken before about identifying deficiencies. We have presented these as resulting from the shortcomings of one-centeredness, automated processes, lack of will, and the accompanying state of non-involvement. The lesson of importance here is to try to recognise what change is needed by viewing situations from a larger perspective. Only a larger collective vision can keep a system from becoming trapped in its own blind automatism.

Summary of the Next Seven Stages of Recovery When Applied to Use in a Company

Stage 1 - It is not always wise to take the highest positions and/or decisions but rather to take the most *fitting* ones. The courage to make such decisions proves that one is not afraid of losing face. In the end, one will (secretly) be highly appreciated and respected for it. Take the position that fits best with one's true goals.

Stage 2 - The only form of enrichment that will not cause imbalance in the world comes forth from an inner preparation (outside of any circumstances), which evaluates what is necessary to *restore harmony* to the environment. Take care of what needs to be taken care of.

Stage 3 - The needs of the moment will decide what is or is not useful for a further evolution. If one posits a norm through misjudgement, it will be broken down. The only place where one remains in control is in a *neutral place* without emotional disturbance and the distraction of limiting thoughts—a

---

further the basic attitude necessary to adapt more fully to reality while creating thereby a better concept of reality and a better sense of how to approach reality via a sensibility that has been reformed and now functions as a more open and realistic organ of perception. The "common Man" represents all that lies between the Ruler and the Fallen Tower (or Fallen Man), his fully reincarnating principle on the direct vertical plane. Once something is brought into life, it is in debt to the principle of the Hanged Man. Here, man is dependent on a learning process for which a teacher may emerge to guide him in the process. This guided "process of becoming" is successful only when it is worked out through the dual coordination of Love and Will. Only when the Love to grow is strong enough can the Will change to its necessary form and succeed in the process. This kind of accompanying Will aspect as it operates in the process can be seen in the diagram below:

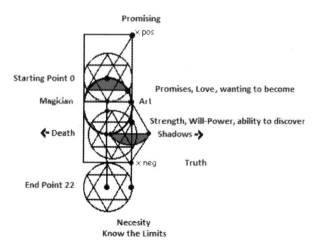

Here, we can see that to discover oneself, an energy of Love is needed to activate the commitment to bring one's elements into circulation. If the desire to make it happen is too demanding from the start—adding too much pressure to the balancing scale and too little of the necessary elements—Death will take over the process. A lack of coherence and insight will likewise add too many unnecessary elements, and a larger "shadow" will emerge (the Devil). The teacher's encouragement to bring elements into circulation that are able to face the recovery process is inspired by a Willpower that first needs the Love (and desire) of the pupil. The teacher's goal, however, is not to express the joy or art of balance alone but to add a degree of awareness that will reveal the elements of integration and order while also exposing their inner limitation and the true shape of necessity.

place where one remains wholly attentive to the needs of each moment. Learn to find that confined place.

Stage 4 - If you feel you are getting involved in things that begin to feel like a matter of "life and death," it is likely that you have become involved in someone else's business and/or processes. Therefore, keep your distance at all times from things that are not your business. This way, each separate evolution can take its own proper course. Mind your own business.

Stage 5 - Don't go criticising and pointing out all that is going wrong in the narrow and imprisoned worlds that you recognise, but instead use this information to understand your own specific world of ideas and values and to restore what is missing in your own little world. This will be inspiring to the extent that you are able to solve things for yourself. Restore things from your own position.

Stage 6 - Realise that imperfections in oneself and in the world have a comparable rhythm. Once one discovers the common desire for solutions that will integrate these things into the rhythm of life, a larger context emerges that works as inspiration for everyone involved in the same affairs. Work with everyone involved together.

Stage 7 - Try to recognise what change is needed by viewing the situation from a larger perspective or a perspective outside one's own. Only a wider and more commonly shared vision keeps a system from becoming trapped in its own blind automatism. Let different perspectives surprise you.

Together, all these rhythmical movements or inclinations indicate good leadership—understood as the knowledge of the rhythms of common situations.

13

THE CONSTANT DOZEN

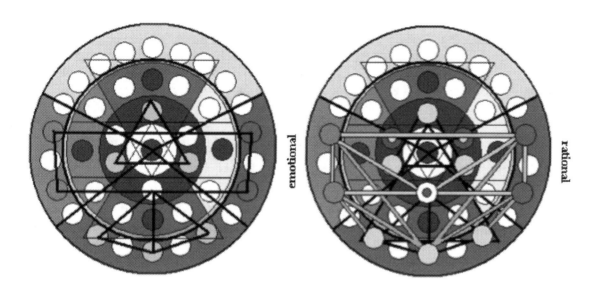

In the above diagrams, we see two green-coloured circles (left-hand side) and two blue-coloured circles (right-hand side), which both result in two "composite energies": an *emotional value* that will be completed by an equivalent *rational value*. Merging the *emotional* (shown on the left in its practical outcome colour of green) with the *rational* (shown on the right and coloured blue) creates at each point (or circle on the diagram) a *neutralisation* of a joint concentration. Through this joint concentration, a new activity or new inspiration is made possible. The nature of these inspirations will be explained through the next twelve phases, which we call here "The Constant Dozen."

The focus now is no longer upon the phase relations of the twenty-two cards in their full activity and dependency but upon the *oppositional points*, which constitute twenty-two "open" spaces functioning as supplementary attainments for the processes of the Minor Arcana. The "neutralised places" of the twenty-two cards are represented by the three lower yellow bulbs in the bottom grey region of the outer circle of the Third Arcana. Through the intersection of the composite energies anticipating completion within a given process, the "expected results" come within reach (as the perfect "answers" to particular situations). Thanks to this process of awareness, the effectiveness resulting from the anticipated situations will begin to work as an active source of inspiration.

At the very least, we can say here that the potential to complete processes is now close at hand. The sense of "discovery" will now be much greater than the sense of "searching." The actual process of integrating the elements involved also ensures that this openness has concrete results within its range. Previously, things coming from the "open" aspect were only sensed as a vague intuition because too many processes and relationships were not yet established. Now, this "openness" is made accessible.

What before had been only pure intuition now becomes the concrete experience of various modes of "higher intelligence." These "modes" function faster and are much more capable of understanding than even the four centres of experience working together. In contrast to the earlier forms of intuition, their results can now be grasped by *all* the bodies of experience *simultaneously*. The processes of the final twelve stages complete the entire process of Becoming Aware. As we will see later, a thirty-third "aspect" can be added, which provides an overview of all the energies harmonically organised and offers a proper perspective of the rhythmic variations of the whole.

Path 21: The "Intelligence of Desire"

Speaking of this stage, Waite remarks, "The twenty-first path is called the Rewarding Intelligence of Those Who Seek." Westcott names this path the "Conciliatory Intelligence." Following the processes of the previous seven phases, one now begins a form of "free work" having begun to understand the whole social context of one's environment. Less and less will one consider the conditions caused by interference from the personality. The choices made now are of a *different order*. One may compare this phase with sight or vision. In this context, "vision" means "looking out for what one may do." In the past, one's desire had been to project, to one degree or another, the immature character of the personality that was seeking to become. Now, desire is experienced as a matter of perception.

Waite, elaborating further on this stage, tells us, "It receives all divine influences and, thanks to its blessings, it influences all existing things." The whole process of awareness begins anew once more. From the point of view of creativity, this awareness now begins as a result of our values being in balance and being observed from a state of openness and neutrality. In the final phases of the Third Arcana, the balance between the emotional and rational possibilities of perception reveals that the choices being made through such perceptions are becoming neutralised in circumstances as well. The tarot card associated with this situation is that of the Empress, who can adapt appropriately to any circumstance. The Empress stands for the type of person who has established a perfect balance between inner and outer needs. This kind of inner balance knows, first, what constitutes weakness in oneself; second, what the weak points are in the corresponding situations; and, third, to what degree this indicates an imperfect phase of development.

At this juncture, one handles situations and social contexts without having to consider oneself—something, which, up until this moment, would not have been the case. Here, the establishment of equilibrium between desires and thoughts permits one to remain open to the unexpected without seeking to do anything. The intelligence now liberated is nourished by the ability to simply "see" what *is* and to articulate that effectively, providing the capacity to evaluate the desires of anyone and everyone. In general, one perceives people as seekers after some kind of purpose or significant meaning who must undergo the same laws one has experienced. The like-minded among them one endeavours to help. One knows that cooperation with a greater number of people will create a more substantial work. Thus, with the "Intelligence of Desire," one is able to support people more easily. The development of vision, of perception, of acuity and depth, from near and from afar, are in fact signs of the possibility of applying a form of depth perception to all situations.

Path 22: The "Faithful or Loyal Intelligence"

In describing this phase, Waite says, "It is the Faithful Intelligence because spiritual values are placed therein and are strengthening themselves until they are transferred to those who live under its shadow." In the "newly discovered quest" previously mentioned are gathered valuable elements from all sorts of moments. The observer here waits patiently until the valuable elements reappear.

In this patient state, the emphasis is no longer placed on "seeing" what exists in a given moment but on "listening" to the circumstances. This phase is therefore associated with *hearing*. For the ordinary person, it is much easier to "listen" to what one recognises or is familiar to. This means that one can only treat others as "equals" when one learns to recognise and becomes familiar with all the issues that they encounter. Practically speaking, "listening" to others involves a *willingness to listen*. In this phase, listening means being able to recognise the "equilibrating energy." Once one has passed through a number of such equilibrating processes, the ability to listen becomes more extensive. Again, it is important to recognise here that everyone is passing through *similar* kinds of processes, albeit with their own specific elements. Just as in the previous phase, the "Intelligence of Desire" was aroused by all that became potentially visible, in this phase the potential of a complete capacity to listen (the receptive attitude) can be developed to the extent that one is able to notice "readiness" and to make something of such readiness regardless of what stage of development it is in. The moment this sort of willingness becomes present the "Loyal Intelligence" forthwith becomes useful.

The tarot card associated with this phase is the Emperor. When this intelligence becomes operative, one realises how to adapt this idea to all situations in all possible ways to obtain the maximum from all situations. In this phase, one had better keep one's eyes and one's ears open. Personal processes are now in subordination to what one sees and hears. For the first time, these communicative skills can be used to the full with a correct and healthy openness without distraction from the imperfections of subservient processes. By increasing the number and degree of distinctions in both one's hearing and one's vision, one learns to make contact with "higher" or more sensitive intelligences, which are no longer the mere products of "desire." In summary, the "Loyal Intelligence" concerns a commitment and openness to the spiritual senses and stands for a "preparedness to listen" that encourages a state of empathy and receptivity.

Path 23: The "Steady Intelligence"

This next phase is associated with the sense of smell or *scent*. Through odour, an even more complex perception can be followed whose range exceeds all previous experiential bodies and senses taken together. One can recognise phases of odour not only in fragrances but also in the amount of willingness a person exudes in a particular field of experience as well as in the amount of "readiness" acquired to bring about a balance between all the phases and the periods of gestation.

Waite refers to this path as "the source of coherence in all numbering." In the ordinary sense, "numberings" usually indicate the different stages in a rhythmical process. Via certain harmonic combinations, "openings" to particular potentials within situations can be achieved. In theory, one can promote certain states and predict and calculate the phases of various rhythmic processes as, for example, in certain Indian rituals through the selection of certain colours, scents, and so forth. The advanced intelligence that can be acquired through smell is extremely quick in sensing such combinations. Obviously, this sense is being used here as a means to consciously interpret the syntheses within a given area. A purely instinctive learning process would only be able to make distinctions of physical or chemical potencies. Through the power of desire and projection, one would be able to distinguish a much greater range of associations and interactions. Conceptually, too, one would also be able to differentiate at least some nuances. But before one is able to use smell as a vehicle for a higher intelligence, one must have passed beyond the phase of projection. There must be some real distance from one's own automatic processes of experience (of the four centres) before one is able to distinguish other processes outside of them. When that finally happens, the experiences will no longer be about reacting automatically to chemical effluvia but about modes of consciousness and the further development of synthesising abilities.

The process of becoming aware of the inspiration activated in this way is disengaged from the situation as soon as one understands the inner meaning of the card the High Priestess. She is the stable centre who knows how to adapt to all situations and can perceive all processes, chemical and "supra-chemical" alike. Unlike the Magician, who is acting directly, she perceives directly before practically carrying out this perception with the patterns foreseen therein. On the ordinary human plane, one departs from the recognition of the like-minded to search for a way to assemble scents. Balance between various kinds of strange combinations becomes the norm to put the working area into activity. Within this balance, the underlying coherence can be stimulated further. This can be done through desire for a stimulus sent through one of the chemical processes. This desire to steer circumstances is one of the reasons why perfumes are made (although in a market context, the true "matches" are not taken into account). Remember, however, that the intelligence of smell remains largely focused on recognising the right combination and not upon forcing a situation. It is able to recognise levels of development. However, rather than adding elements—remember that this intelligence functions from stability—it reveals the elements that are natural and with which all present processes can be stabilised, neutralised, and vitalised again.

Path 24: The "Imaginative Intelligence"

Originally, it was the role of language to indicate *forms of directional change*. The basic tones of nature lie in the rhythms of her evolutionary movement. Animals "honour" these phases through their expressions. In its earliest manifestations, human language was little more than the merging of certain combinations of these same rhythms, coupled with a projection of the direction in which our human bodies of experience were evolving. At a certain stage, a coded knowledge began to accumulate, and a more extensive form of language began to emerge. Gradually, this latter development focused on expressing the innate directional principals latent therein.

Some Middle Eastern languages still retain these kinds of "declarations of direction" and use these directional modes in the formation of certain words and sentences. Some sound combinations in these languages are still used to declare the directions in which certain processes evolve. Many of the original "God Names" have their root in these "directions." Unfortunately, for the sake of one-centeredness (with the used idea of one opinion and direction fits all), the different names for these creative directions (or functional indicators) today are only vaguely subsumed under the one word "God." This generalised anthropocentric projection has become so diluted over the centuries that it now lacks any vital connection with its original purpose of sound-meaning-based direction. The result of this lamentable state of affairs is that such processes are barely sensed any more. What is important for our present discussion is that every detail that has come forth from the development of language once had the purpose of setting up a number of possibilities for the direction of thought, logic, and expression.

This kind of language code gradually permitted the human being to project all the rhythmic processes of his or her experiential body into this new form of expression—with the additional ability to gain some degree of distance from the process. Much of this wonderful art of understanding how these directions work whilst maintaining recognition of the consequences of directing it this way or that way has unfortunately degenerated into a vague recollection of orientation. The possibilities of this great art and science have been reduced to a secondary tool for expression, which consists of little more than a degraded form of association. Some of the original words once associated with "important directions" have been retained, but these for the most part have become vague forms, which are now little more than religious and literary clichés. The usefulness of the content of such forms became dogmatised until at last they appeared as mere vestiges of a memory to which modern man had lost the key. Today, language is now used predominantly for the orientation of mental and emotional streams of thought and is much less concerned with *vital orientation*.

The recovery of the "lost language" is concerned with restoring the essence of natural directions using key words as anchors. The secret of the method of the primordial animation of words was a simple, direct approach intimately connected to the senses and centres of the human organism. In certain Judaic traditions, it has even become the custom to no longer use the "names of God"—names whose meanings were once considered to exist on much higher spheres of the Kabbalistic Tree. Such attitudes surely close the door to the spontaneous developments of such directions. In the Christian tradition, the situation is even worse. All existing "names of God" are subsumed under one word: "God." How the mind and heart may be oriented by such a summary and simplification "God" only knows!

We may fruitfully compare the ability to "listen" to words with the ability to listen to music. Take someone with a poorly developed musical ear—that is to say, someone with a limited listening faculty. Such a person will coordinate his perceptions of words in a similar manner to the way he experiences music. A musical ear develops in proportion to its sensitivity. When the listening faculty is of a primitive type, a person cannot even follow the simplest of rhythms. For the more sensitive and experienced ear that is sensitised with the appropriate "antennae," there is a greater possibility of his or her being "in tune" with the possibilities of the world, of distinguishing certain compositions, and adding to them something of his or her own perspective. In this respect, language is no different. For whosoever can grasp deeper layers of intelligence behind the logic expressed and known through language will possess greater distinctions as soon as this kind of intelligence begins to flower.

Through spoken language, the whole of the imagination can be projected and channelled. Today, people still associate *speech* with the imaginative intelligence, while the structure of language itself, its grammatical and logical order, still maintains its own inherent form of logic, which can become a secondary source of inspiration for one's thought processes. However, the preference for this kind of logic and method possesses a bias towards certain types of thought processes. Clearly, there exist many more types of processes that cannot be put into simple and common language. At a certain stage, sensitivity to the perception of this truth might be more important than the pre-prepared known language to get to the object of perception. Yet there still remain numerous possibilities yet undiscovered within language itself.

Waite's description of this path suggests that any form of language is a form of mutual agreement chosen for communication, developing details of physical movement and types of sensory behaviour and directions. Thus, he says, "It causes the agreement in the likeness of beings created in accordance with its aspects." Speech can be used not only as a tool for various forms of logic and to indicate various directions of the mind but also to project all sorts of opportunities into a separate interactive work field before implementing them in reality. From there, it can build something in advance without having to first experience the matter physically. This particular phase refers to the meaning of the tarot card Strength (or Force). It refers to all kinds of situations where one is able to adjust oneself to circumstances through the application of the right measure and proportion. What happens here is that Force projects the potentials that are within outwards upon the physical and observable world. "Speech" is used as the *sum total of the imagination* a person uses for such implementation.

What is necessary at this juncture is a quality of personal feeling for the deeper language of awareness itself, of how it makes connections between specific differences, and then uses these to switch into a communicative process that connects those aspects. The capacity to organise imagination in a proficient way provides the power to create a working area. He who only repeats events as events is not using the "Intelligence of Imagination." This principle and the inspiration that comes with the tarot card Force conceives of the experimental field as a *direct form of projection.*[13]

---

[13] In volume 2, we will go deeper into this matter and explain further that spoken and written language need not only be sensed via a mental projection of thoughts. Deeper levels are possible, which come close to the origins of language via intonation and "rebuses of direction." In volume 2, we will explain all the combinations of the word *taro*, which refer to certain key moments in the development of the tarot, indicating changes and directions in the modus operandi of its metabolic processes.

Path 25: The "Intelligence of Temptation or Trial"

At this stage, a lot more communicative possibilities are becoming available to the perceptive field and working area. However, this does not mean that all the available possibilities and their combinations are necessarily activated and used. Hence, the last and still incomplete phase leads to a further principle of activation or inspiration presented by the tarot card Temperance (a card we have elsewhere called Art and Moderation).

The meaning of this tarot Arcanum stands for the ability in all circumstances to effectively to balance and coordinate one thing with another. Together with the "Intelligence of Temptation or Trial," the actual and true mentality, which has been built up during the coordination of the targets, will now come forth. This path is also called the "Path of Eating and Drinking," with a focus on food and drink, and not on "taste" (as one might expect when led by the senses). Taste itself is much more bound to the personality and is therefore less of a neutral guide. It is only a passive subject. On the other hand, the choice of food selected is the active substance one works with. What is it that one really wants and that one desires to feed further? The intelligence that comes to one's aid at this stage is provoked by the spirit of moderation. If one is able to observe facts in a neutral way and with the necessary distance, exaggerated elements can be compensated for not only through temperance but also through the use of the right supplement until eventually one succeeds in reconciling the larger contradictions.

In Dutch, the word for "sinful" has the secondary connotation of "shameful." This is exactly how one ought to view the word in English too. It is helpful to look upon "sin" as something "shameful" in the sense of being something that causes *sadness* and *misfortune*—through certain elements becoming excessive. Of course, the existence of strange excesses does not mean that one's true motives might not have started out as pious. Consider the case of Rasputin, who may have learned to reconcile his contradictions in later life had he been given more time. The methods and images that he used were those belonging to a path and a belief system that was common in his time, one that encouraged the development of extreme opposites so that they might come to a creative synthesis. This is a life choice and a "Path."

Piety cannot be recognised by a formal standard but only through the faith, the trust, and the kind of commitment that is being put into something (whether it proves "successful"). Who are we to judge? When Waite states here that this is "the first temptation by which God tests the righteous," be reminded that it is nearly impossible to directly recognise a person's true intentions behind a form of excess. With regard to the notion of "eating and drinking," we may note here a particular association of Temperance with food. The old adage "You are what you eat" is to some extent true since the elements one incorporates become part of a further development of one's own gestation. A person who has certain "chemical triggers" takes the risk that certain resilient units or bases will thereby be affected. One's resilience or defence system has much more to do with food, being fed and the ability to feed certain processes, than it has to do with physical resistance. The importance of "food," of being fed, and being able to nourish, cannot be underestimated. What Temperance here suggests and, indeed, what the entire goal of the whole recovery process indicates is that through *metabolism*, everything becomes more workable, useful, and in the end will find its place in the system.

Path 26: The "Renewing Intelligence"

This phase is associated with the tarot card Love or the Lovers (a card that we have also named the Beloved and exemplifies the Principle of Exchange). The situation here emerges from the previous stage. Imagine someone who still continues to accept all temptations in life. These temptations will offer this person the opportunity to put certain aspects into circulation and to unfold them further. This is a much easier approach than that of the person who constantly fights and resists temptations and fails to move forward in life from one year to the next.

When all of this is released via a path of developmental transformation, the situation becomes something other than a primitive frustration. The tarot card that proposes a solution to this dilemma is called the Lovers—that is to say, the *exchange principle* that exists between people. The willingness to share something—regardless of the risk involved in doing so—strengthens not only the well-developed aspects of the self but also the underdeveloped ones. If one's aim is for improvement, this leaves one open to renewal from the inside out.

Two worlds projected upon one another get the chance for renewal through the elements that come together in this way. The intelligence that is hereby activated through this "shared situation" is called the "Innovative or Renewing Intelligence" because it provides a new opportunity for a number of elements. This intelligence can only become fully available when one learns to apply the exchange principle within all kinds of situations. This phase is also called the "Path of the Coitus" because here one experiences how sex and unification can truly innovate and improve elements through exchange. While ordinary sexuality as presented by the media remains linked with the previous principles of Strength (or Lust) embracing Temptation, the actual result of sexuality goes much further and deeper according to the nature of what one is able to *share*. The "result" can deliver a certain fusion of rhythmic elements in such a way that supports and conjoins the fates involved. This is about much more than simple Tantric techniques. Someone who consciously experiences this process and who has shared much "love" knows that one's personality can be completely renewed by another's vital rhythms. Such a person knows it takes time and attention to remain inspired by the joint potential of these innovative opportunities.

Even "outsiders" are able to detect the effects of this increased potential when elements are reconciled. "Reconciliation" is one form of exchange, but there exist others. Temptation is only the beginning of an initiative to spontaneously test the conditions. The exchange process of love and lovers creates the *vital moment* that, according to the degree of commitment of all the capacities involved, creates exceptional opportunities. The degree to which one knows the rhythmically activated potentialities in oneself and experiences harmony with them—both rationally and emotionally so that a complete openness through them becomes possible—is the basis for an exchange via a "neutral initiative." This automatically creates a certain willingness to share. As soon as there exists the "match" to share a similar number of elements, this will be transmitted by the chemistry activated through the state of openness. Whenever a chemical reaction emerges, this activates an additional energy, which in turn neutralises a certain portion of the reaction and activates a surplus of new kinds of composites.

Not only basic chemistry but also supra-chemical processes can trigger these kinds of progressions. The more one is conscious of oneself, the greater will be the overall effects of the chemical provocations. Where sexuality is concerned, only those elements will be activated that manage to find a "match." These elements can be activated precisely because there exist stimulating links between them. In the absence of any "match," however, certain potencies are forced to abort. In the case of masturbation, which in some cultures is considered a sin, this may mean—for men especially—a kind of neutralisation of energies that might otherwise remain active for too long. If these energies fail to get channelled, they can in certain cases take on excessive values. Thus, a deliberate mental concentration upon the neutralising aspects of such activated energies may prove useful in providing a new working area. Outside of this, there also exist certain methods of channelling energy, which are used in place of masturbation and partake of the aid of the "will." Remember that whatever method one selects to finish something or work something out, the most practical aspect of it continues to watch over the neutral point of concentration in which what is projected can be renewed. This is not so much a matter of reasoning as a sense of feeling that focuses the mind.

The "common elements" mentioned above consist of a specific sum of all four experiential centres working together as a form of harmonic synthesis produced through a "match." The "chemistry" that is engaged through the operation of common elements provides a signal that stimulates a person in such a way that something more than the fulfilment of desire alone can be exchanged. This type of exchange is obviously very difficult for persons whose experience of sexual exchanges has occurred through force and domination and not through love. It is likely that in such circumstances, the exchange has been marked by an exposure to primitive and base tendencies, and the chemistry that does emerge remains disturbed in its functioning. This may cause it to abort the development of certain processes leading to feelings of despair and unhappiness. In India, astrological conditions are consulted to determine if persons share *complementary elemental conditions* (or harmonic "matches") to avoid the conflict and contradiction that may characterise the frustrating exchanges that often result from forced marriages.

Of course, a real exchange only happens with someone when one feels that the other has many abilities—even when these include very different capacities to one's own. This is one of the lessons to be learned from the card the Beloved. In the description of this tarot card, it was made clear that its value is not solely concerned with the exchange that takes place between two people but refers to all manner of exchanges.

Path 27: The "Natural Intelligence"

The Arcanum, which shows the conditions for "Natural Intelligence," is the tarot card Justice, a card that elsewhere we have given the secondary title "Balancing out Coincidences." In simple terms, this card is about *discernment*. Justice means being able to recognise, attend to, and make distinctions concerning shifts in the balance between things. Here, one can be certain that the elements are present within the joint ellipse and will certainly finish their process and be brought into association with the "Natural Intelligence." Through this intelligence, Waite explains, "The nature of anything that is in orbit around the sun is completed and perfected."

This refers to all processes, individual or collective, that can be accomplished within one complete cycle. On the other hand, one could say that a lasting partnership exists whenever a joint cycle has commenced. Everyone and everything has its own kind of cycle—whether it be a project, a contract, an agreement or business—that needs to be conceptualised further in this way.

One can compare this Arcanum with the astrological sign of Libra, indicating the scales applied to all situations, applying the natural art of assessment. Westcott refers to this phase as the "Exciting Intelligence." The nature of the "excitement" is probably due to the freed enthusiasm and increased energy that occurs when everything is progressing harmoniously and there are few obstacles. The continuous motion of the process is now the only strict requirement. In this way, the process continues to muster enthusiasm. Sometimes, this phase is also spoken of as "the Path of Work." It is through work that this inspiration finds its essential expression. The "Libra point" refers to the point of *neutrality* one adopts in changing circumstances. The changes in circumstances themselves do not influence this concept.

Path 28: The "Tactile or Active Intelligence"

This next phase is associated with the Wheel of Fortune. Herein, favourable occasions occur that bring numerous opportunities for moments of synchronisation or "openings" that make possible new events. Both fortune and misfortune must be understood as being grounded in the same opportunities that arise to offer certain matters the chance for exchange. This stage concerns the increasing possibilities of *subsequent* "meeting places"—that is to say, places where more and more potentially varied material is being deployed.

The purpose of increasing the number of occasions for such openings allows for the release or activation of certain patterns. Whenever such occasions occur, the possibilities within them will be seen as new potentials. The degree of enthusiasm this arouses is drawn from the fact that one knows beforehand that a coincidence is likely and that it is viable and that one has the energy and requisite commitment necessary to respond to it. This phase is also called "the Path of Movement." One might also add here that it is the path of being *set in motion* or of being encouraged to act. It would not be without advantage to use this opportunity to "dance"—that is to say, to play with the movements and in this way channel all the activities that are differently disposed within the various bodies of experience.

At this juncture, more or less everything is put into action.

Path 29: The "Physical Intelligence"

The only way to adapt quickly enough to all the changes happening, in the totality of movement, is via the Body. Before realising the true control centre behind all the processes (and engagements) of movement, this area is first realised by receipt of challenging impulses impinging upon the emotional and rational sensory organ separately. This happens in an area in which instinctive reaction patterns half-automatically respond mostly either emotionally or rationally. Because these processes are half-automatic, at that stage, the adjusting operations are open to suggestion. Situations in which to react can be provoked in which one of both centres can be heavily challenged when facing contradictions. Up to this stage, it can become one of man's weakest spots. Through opposing weakness in situations, all weak energies will be thrown off their pedestal, showing their deficiency. At that stage, an extra alertness and readiness is activated, mobilising and exposing all true stages of growth towards matured conditions.

This stage is often referred to as the "Path of Wrath." Leaving aside the apparently negative connotations of this name, let us try to put the associations into a much wider context. Instead of interpreting the "Path of Wrath" in terms of some malicious form of revenge, we may instead consider the opportunity for revenge as a useful function, one that enables us to reverse certain energies predominating in our centres or in the daily reality of situations. The tarot card associated with this path is the (Falling) Tower—a phase that we have described elsewhere as the Tribulation, referring as it does so to a test that serves to clarify the true energy that one is deliberately putting into something to maintain its activity. If one properly understands the lessons of the Tower, one now knows that the personality and the solitariness that adhere to it still remain subordinate to the amount of dedicated effort put into things.

Following confrontation, what will be usefully mobilised is what stands firm and is grounded. If it is not grounded (at each moment, in each demanded position), it will fall. This feeling of strength will be found in one's "body" through a "physical stance." This is not so much about self-assuredness but about firmness of being, remaining capable of mobilising further any exposed weak energies as a

163

workable tool. The way in which this form of developing movement communicates is through a more "physical" mode of being than via a first reaction from a rational or emotionally central point of view. It is especially and only through the mobilisation of this new unifying organ that one is able to improve any existing imbalances.

In an organisation (or a body) like a company, it is necessary to focus upon this energy every so often when dealing with employees so that the overall growth will not stagnate. There are no excuses left for those who refuse to partake in its processes. If excuses are noticed, this is the moment to include additional training or retraining or swift changes of position. At this stage, persons in "unlawfully acquired" positions must be confronted with the overall inflexibility of their movements. People who continue to fail at this stage should look for something else. What is expected from this "physical stance" is true commitment. Certain positions require certain movements. Here, they will be checked if people in such positions can also handle the required commitment.

Because all will express itself most clearly through the direct appearance of one's bodily attitude, it is never without value to stimulate the mobility of the nodes in the body. An increasing mobility in all the nodes is able to restore the full capacity to properly "ground" oneself. This permits one to focus better on all one's bodily experiences without experiencing automated restrictions. A lack of adequate "grounding" is largely due to a lack of practical capacity or to a lack of true connection between certain parts of our bodies of experience. This also refers to the different parts in the body that correspond to the origin of one of the senses. The more movement made possible between the senses, the more processes become involved in digesting and activating further the totality of events.[14]

In this phase, the focus is on what one needs to improve practically. If in reality you behave in a weak, impractical, and inflexible way, now is the time to work on these deficiencies. A focus on such things is a test of one's resilience. The "Physical Intelligence" focuses especially on one's immediate behaviour and direct practice and not upon the idealistic notions occurring in one's head or heart. It may be the case that certain people have been patient with you in the past and have been perennially accepting off the rigidity of your actions. Now is the time for such rigidity to disappear. Sooner or later, actions that are impractical have to be adjusted. Such is the law.

One can also learn to loosen all of the knots or areas in the body via *movement*. By increasing one's mobility directly through the body, more energies will be permitted to flow freely. Stiffness in the body often correlates to stiffness in relationships. Mobilising the limbs and spine mobilises inherent conflicts; mobilising the shoulders and the pelvis activates desires and emotional and digestive circulations; mobilising the neck stimulates the head; and so on.

A fine example of the way in which suggestion can mobilise the centres, when remaining too much in separation, can be found in one of Gurdjieff's talks on hypnotism, which refers to how the connections between the different centres can be disconnected and a person become subject to influence, rendered dependent, or severely weakened.[15]

Says Gurdjieff,

> The complexities of the methods of hypnotism are determined by the number of possible combinations. There are connections between all centres. In man's waking state either the thinking or the emotional

---

[14] In volume 2, we will provide several simple examples of movements aimed at mobilising the body (from the point of view of the O-Fool), which will stimulate the working together of head (ratio), trunk (heart), pelvis (instinct), and the use of the limbs to unite these various elements of experience in practice.

[15] From a student's recollection of a talk delivered in Tiflis in 1919.

centre is always active, which the other, as it were, observes and criticises so as not to allow it to commit "stupidities." If there is no connection—which means there is no criticism or censorship—the man will do anything the centre active at that moment happens to wish, which means he will commit many "stupidities" on sight. The task of the hypnotist consists in breaking artificially for a time this connection and then in giving commands to one of the centres which will then carry out everything literally, since there will be no criticism on the part of the other centre. For an explanation of the connection between centres it is useful to repeat the comparison, already given, of the human machine with a team consisting of carriage, horse, and driver. The connection between centres may be compared with the reins and the shafts . . . When the hypnotist breaks the (right) connection, he tells the patient to do this and that and, since criticism of the other centre is absent, the patient believes him and does as he is told. Even if the other centre sees that something is not as it should be it can do nothing and can change nothing for, owing to the broken connection, it can send no commands to that centre.

Gurdjieff goes on to describe a second method in this discussion that refers to the general irradiation of a person's atmosphere, the rays of an emanation or *direction of desire* through which the energy of a stronger will and focus can act upon a weaker one and transfer certain ideas or emotions to the latter. In this case, the signals can reach the centre of desire more directly via a bodily reaction. This example is really referring to the degree of unity of will one must attempt to achieve. Losing such coordination and control over the emotional and rational centres can, of course, happen on much grander scales as, for example, in the case of large groups being influenced. In the latter, for instance, rational ideas are blurred via generalising emotional negative responses. The process in investigating what really needs to change at the moment, checking also the intentions behind any manipulated directions, in that case the process has been replaced by feeding personal needs for an emotional response.

Therefore, I have said before that it is always important to "stand firm" to keep control over what exactly it is that needs developing and engagement. However, I have sadly noticed that this explanation of the importance of "standing firm" could still easily work confusing for those types of persons who still have based their own engagement mainly upon dealing with and tending to fall back mostly on responding only positively on all confirming impulses of what they know so far. What will be needed next is the realisation that there exist moments of challenge that will show one's true direct practical commitment, which is put into one's own generalised stance. This commitment can be found and is reflected at the same time in one's general bodily structural stance, which at times will be forced to be blown away from its safe balance through confrontation or impulses of contradiction; at such points, it will always show its true structural integrity of flexibility and ability to adapt fluently, in response to all what is needed in terms of mobilisation towards the whole/the outside/the responding world or by any opposite positions that demand a different kind of movement or a certain form of changing shape. The true "steadily" adaptation can be felt and learned half-automatically by feeling more closely the mobilisation processes needed via the fascial structure in the body. In that way, the steady aspect will be much more related with the firmness in one's engagement in whatever shape is needed at any given moment. Such adapting reflection is *no* longer centred on a mental condition but is much more directly related to one's firm attitude of commitment. Here, one starts to notice how much one's body is able to correspond and adapt well to change and that this bodily container truly reflects the main steering organ for it, because through it, one can react and adapt more quickly towards what is needed, via any change of focus, much more quickly than with any other sensory organ separately. If, for instance, one focuses on one's thoughts alone that get out of balance by a needed change of focus, a person rationally tends to fall back on stubbornness. If at such situations of need one merely focuses on one's emotions, its blockages and emotional resistance will be felt most. Remaining separated, the emotional or rational centres can't handle such confusions alone and can no longer find ways to participate further into the steering processes and will merely react blindly with a coward reaction of retreat, while reality demanded a more willingly change of attitude. The same impulses given when being felt from here when seen from the mobile bodily structure, these reactions will no longer be open so easily either to suggestion (from outside) or to refusal to adapt further with flexibility (from inside), but will be able to adapt further to one's own full engagement without reacting half-automatically but in a more controlled way of feeling the further need how to finalise all activities, restoring further what has shown itself already in imbalance, with the further help of now more cooperative senses, via a firmness of being.

The next step will require us to further penetrate into the existence of all of the activity available and bring it into a larger collective.

Path 30: The "Collective Intelligence"

Eventually, the group energy itself will be found to be most decisive. If one could draw directly from this group energy that steers the totality of changes, one would be able to draw upon a much larger number of possibilities and combinations of phases and rhythms than would ever be possible from the contribution of one individual alone. The energy mobilised via group movements is more decisive in carrying out compatible solutions. This is not solely about the collaborative energies that bind people but about the chance factors that play a vaster role in the game and whose influence increases the kinds of openings that can be made possible.

To understand how to properly apply the Fool within any situation is to predict how, in its own manner of responding, it relates to "chance" by paying attention to latent patterns. The "Collective Intelligence" is what focuses upon the common features. This phase is also called the "Path of Joy" in contradistinction to the previous "Path of Wrath," which cleared away the obstructions allowing for a better fluency among all processes. The major disadvantage of the Fool is that he is fully dependent on all the conditions that have been created. On the other hand, the advantage of his role is that the Fool is able to open up each of these circumstances without anyone being able to stop him from doing so. Yet because the Fool represents All and Everything, his role can be stimulating for the needs of each instant.

Waite compares this phase with the inspiration used by astrologers in their study of the stars prior to assessing and predicting the character of events. The intelligence and inspiration of *The Fool Who Has Become Wise* makes him a specialist in adapting perfectly to the demands of any situation. The path associated with this inspiration is that of *merriment*. While in the previous phases one might have worked against situations maintaining various excuses and still becoming very unhappy when situations didn't turn out as one had expected or predicted, in this phase all situations will be perceived in advance as being advantageous because one senses the collective need in each situation, working with nature to make everything happen just as it must. At this stage, all lessons have been learned. This Fool knows that everything is exactly as it should be.

Path 31: The "Continuing Intelligence"

When all the previous stages are taken together, a realisation emerges that each essence will have its own time and place. Although each phase will at some point completely disappear as a form that makes it survive within a cycle will remain a much more powerful aspect. It would be very unfortunate if the knowledge of a larger unity disappeared from the collective memory. Human kind would then lose all the completed essences within that unity such as, for instance, is the case regarding those essences that used to be transferred as knowledge via an oral transmission. Yet it is a fact that this sort of doleful scenario has happened in the past and indeed will continue to happen in the future. Fortunately, there still remain some basic guiding principles that, acting together in the form of a composite, function like the essence of a "higher mind" capable of summarising the lower elements in a single concept (in a single word with layers of depth). For those who have been encouraged by methods that attempt to provoke the depth in things—such as the methods that once constituted the fundamentals of speech—such persons know that behind the Logos and the logic of language exist other modes of thinking that are capable of grasping these "essences" much quicker. In reality, these essences are not (and cannot) ever be truly lost.

This phase is associated with the tarot card the Hermit. A Hermit (or loner) does not attempt to change what *is* but rather observes the processes that are progressing in a totality. This is also called the "Path of Meditation." Meditation is primarily a slow-motion mode of perception that allows one to perceive and understand processes from the *inside*. By activating the consciousness that is behind every kind of essence meditation encourages the essences to "become" in their totality. From this point of view, it is as if the light of understanding distinguishes the issues in any given situation through finding out that they have an essence of their own, which permits them to move on and complete their cycle. It is this kind of power that meditation possesses. One of the names of this path, the "Continual Intelligence," is thus perfectly apt. In connection with this phase, let us not bring in the fashionably foolish fads of quantum loops and such like. Before such naive reasoning comes to the boil, let us strive to understand this idea of the continuation of what cannot be immediately grasped better within its own context. The "observed thing" plays only a small part in the process of evolution being merely an element inside the process of perception. This observation process is the basis of the guiding consciousness that transmits itself further through all chemical and supra-chemical processes. It is because we respond to what we are concerned about that this perception has such a large impact on how each of us reacts. Within the body, consciousness holds together the chemical processes with a life-giving energy, so that its elements will not be too quickly broken down into its own materiality. In that way, consciousness is always in collaboration with our own perception field. Waite says that this path is called the *Continuing Intelligence* "because it governs the movement of the Sun and Moon according to their composition and makes each of them move according to its own orbit."

This last statement puts our previous ones into perspective. Consciousness in the above context clearly requires working with the inborn regularity of its own elements. It is obviously not possible for consciousness to simply transcend every materiality and law. Consciousness itself must follow the pre-programmed rhythms of nature. These pre-programmed rhythms are basically the paths of least resistance and therefore are always associated with the simplest cyclic laws.

What happens at this stage is that we learn to deal with what we cannot see or immediately understand and are simply prepared to deal with it and open our consciousness to it. In a way, we learn to deal with all the existing elements we cannot yet grasp with words, emotional responses, or instinctive directions.

Path 32: The "Assisting Intelligence"

The provision of a deeper look into all that happens is explained in this "final" stage, which is associated with the tarot card Judgement, also known as the Last Judgement (or the AEON), referring to the phase in which *reuse* is a distinct possibility. Unlike the previous phase where one's focus was concerned with the kind of essences that occur in repetitive forms within all cycles and are interspersed with their own formats and detailed phases, one now focuses on the fluency of the entire state of affairs, in other words, on the *wave function* of life and the life function of the wave. One here *becomes* the cycle and is taken into and adapted by it. One willingly surrenders to it. It is simply and completely a "being one" with what *is*. From a certain point of view, this could seem like the ultimate form of servility, consciousness "asleep," and simply performing what it is told to do.

However, the truth is that an underlying principle of subordinate perfection is inherent to this phase. The difference regarding how it is experienced is made by the degree and quality of involvement. It is not "bad" or servile to be "used" by all the chemical and supra-chemical stimuli so that one's consciousness can hold all these processes in balance. What makes the real difference here is that consciousness has now become aware of its own functioning. In this phase, the contradictory processes are able to find rest to restore themselves (something that already happens in normal sleep) in which the initiated processes of bodily experiences are seeking to recover their balance. Consciousness still plays a role here. In fact, the consciousness referred to as the "Assisting Intelligence" is able to follow this process and to assist it like a profound form of meditation. Thus, the whole can renew itself fully from the inside.

A technique one might wish to use in this phase is to concentrate consciousness in the sleep phase. Before going to sleep, let your specific goals and ideas penetrate into this sleep phase, concentrating upon it in such a way that you will still be able to remember this on waking up the following morning. In the meantime, during the sleep phase, the ideas will have been thoroughly worked through, and a dissolved form will emerge to express the essence of the experience having passed through the full cycle of the underlying process. The goal in each occasion is to learn to focus on the next phases that are truly needed. This technique works rapidly in the hunt for solutions and can be applied in a similar manner throughout the day.

It is hoped that the passage through these 110 phases has assisted the reader in putting his elements in balance. Everything is always in motion. If everything is in the right place, then the movement will have a similar shape and in this way will confirm the old adage "As above, so below."

Summary of the Last Twelve Coordinating Stages of Recovery When Applied to Use in a Company

Stage 21 - Take a look and observe clearly all that you have available.
Stage 22 - Look out for what and/or who can be useful. Discover which people are prepared and who among them show a readiness to participate in work. Listen to their ideas.
Stage 23 - Recognise all the stages of development, all the different nuances involved, and recognise what is viable in them or where a viable place can be found for them.
Stage 24 - Articulate and communicate everything as clearly as possible so that all that needs to be said and heard is understood in all its nuances.
Stage 25 - Do not rush to conclusions that the purpose of extravagant effusions of a personal persuasion can be so easily understood. These will often be judged too easily. The question is, Can these (really) nourish us?
Stage 26 - United forces are capable of creating renewing conditions.
Stage 27 - Use all your useful concepts so that they can find new applications and opportunities.
Stage 28 - Put everything you have into motion.
Stage 29 - Mobilise everybody and everything. Change the positions of persons according to the qualities required. To finalise projects, sometimes it is easier to do so from a change and different position.
Stage 30 - Deal, in a complete way, with the directions shown by a general change of situation or group.
Stage 31 - Handle those things that are omnipresent, that you cannot grasp more specifically, but that are nevertheless sensibly present.
Stage 32 - Always follow the general stream of all that comes to life.

Final Summary of the Thirty-Two Intelligences

Following a direct process of confrontation with everything in the Major Arcana, what happens in the first ten stages of awareness is a process of deepening one's experience with the Minor Arcana. This constitutes a learning process concerned with individual progress. One becomes more engaged in a process of filtering out and purifying one's personal impulses in relation to general conditions, and one begins to prepare an attitude capable of acting within a group. What one discovers in these ten stages will be used for such further integration.

The Ten Transcendent States of Awareness

Via the four Aces or the "Mystical Intelligence," one begins to realise that what is needed at the present moment simply comes to one.

Via the four 2s or the "Intelligence of Illumination," one learns to see where everything needs to proceed to.

Via the four 3s or the "Sanctifying Intelligence," one starts to realise that everything and everyone will find their own appropriate place and their own rhythmical processes.

Via the four 4s or the "Receiving Intelligence," one realises that each inner developing centre has its own way of receiving and developing impulses while still working within and towards a common goal.

Via the four 5s or the "Radical Intelligence," the need emerges to focus more upon the practical goals of the main group and to define more clearly the characteristics needed for its common conditions. With better-defined common goals, one realises one is able to make the distinction between these and more personal expressions and limitations.

Via the four 6s or the "Intelligence of Separated Appearance," one is still able to accept and find a place for one's personal paths that continue to play in the background.

Via the four 7s or the "Hidden Intelligence," one limits one's attention to the useless elements and only focuses upon those elements of utilitarian interest.

Via the four 8s or the "Perfect Intelligence," one learns to be open to the above kind of impulses, which one now learns to adapt further to maintain them like a profoundly realistic basis from which to work.

Via the four 9s or the "Purified Intelligence," one learns to instinctively focus on the full picture of reality, which, in its totality, is the most practical reality to work with. Even though this full picture does not follow any known or common rules, it deserves most of our attention. It is especially to this mode of awareness that we need to adapt everything that follows.

Via the four 10s and the "Glorious Intelligence," one is able to show a good example towards others. In the further coordination of one's own impulses, one is no longer mixing things with any of one's personal preferences. One knows that the practicality of the whole will automatically reveal itself.

The Awareness of the Perfect 3

Via the Devil or the "Fiery Consciousness,"[16] one learns that every impulse is a useful one because it reveals a need and will to become.

Via the World or the "Consciousness of Transparency," one begins to recognise the order of all the impulses that seek to become from the world and from each person. With more imagination given to them, things will become more realisable.

Via the Magician and the "Consciousness of the Conduit," one learns that the controlling processes of mankind are governed especially by the mental process of becoming. Therefore, one should always first look for a good articulation.

The next step is concerned with realising the conditions in which all impulses are governed by circumstances in which something becomes or fails to become realised. Instead of focusing on the practical working out of impulses themselves, one begins now to realise the signs of certain conditions and to deal with their nature appropriately—that is to say, in a way that does not disturb their inner or outer evolutionary processes. It shows the manifestation of reality with all its impulses and signals and how any imbalance in them can be neutralised via a specific sort of process of recovery. In each phase, one learns to deal with certain contradictory impulses concerning decisions about what should or cannot become.

The Awareness[17] of the Sacred and Conflicting 7

Via the Sun or the "Awareness of Light," one becomes aware how any evolutionary process once initiated includes its own aspects of *wisdom* as well as its degrees of *folly*. Behind the becoming of each process is the intention to restore the conditions during its preceding formation. In the process of becoming, this gives different perspectives according to the potentiality of the moment.

Via the Moon or the "Constituent Awareness," one realises that the result of each process includes an aspect of *wealth* as well as *poverty*. It contains the awareness that it is not necessary that everything becomes immediately or develops in the same way. It is better for certain things to be more fully prepared via an inner process of development. Any outer development should in fact be limited by its immediate usefulness.

Via the Chariot or the "Eternal Awareness," one realises that *fertility* also includes *destruction*. The previous realisation is developed into a larger context with the understanding that not everything remains effective over time and one should limit oneself to creating a place of neutrality.

Via Death or the "Sensible/Decision Intelligence," one realises that each *life* also includes *death*. Some things cannot be forced to appear before the light. It is also the realisation of how to maintain a distance from things that demand a different type of action.

---

[16] The word "intelligence" comes forth from an ability to perceive and to understand something. For these three coordinating stages, the word "consciousness" is much more appropriate than intelligence. This intelligence depends more fully on your own attitude and needed realisation of its essence before one can mobilise this form of awareness and see where it automatically leads to.

[17] These phases are mostly much more forms of awareness, dependent on what is revealed. Intelligence here is the result, not a source of inspiration. These stages, which I now call more appropriately awareness, are all about what is directly revealed and understood well in its own context. Only in the last stage, one's own participation in such open-minded setting becomes fully integrated and also fully engaged.

Via the High Priest and the "Radiating Awareness or House of influence," one realises how every form of *domination* also includes *slavery*. This is connected with awareness of one's own limited perspective and in which areas one has gained experience and in which areas one has not.

Via the Star and the "Awareness of the Secret of Spiritual Activities," one realises how *peace* is combined with an aspect of *misfortune*. Every condition of peace is capable of including numerous forms of misfortune when it tries to compensate by restoring common rhythms and goals. Peace should not be seen as a situation that segregates itself from the world's movements but as something that encompasses the irregular situations and that awaits openly to the possibilities of change.

Via the Hanged Man and the "Consciousness of the Will," one realises every form of *grace* includes a form of *ugliness*—one adapts to larger energies, groups, and situations to see things from a joint perspective. At this point, having passed through all the other phases, there emerges a will to do something from a neutralised vision via a willingness to recognise, articulate, realise, and develop a vision that can distil all that is useful.

From the combined workings of all these states of awareness, one will receive the sort of impulses not only to enable an understanding of the inevitability of the situations but also when balance can and will be restored as a former of inner realisation.

In the last phase of this series, the impulses that were inhabited to show any undeveloped stages before, because of shying away of its full reality of aspects, after full acceptance of its own rhythm of stages of appearance, they will now more directly be leading you towards a process of a more useful guidance. All impulses felt will now become fully engaged in which you yourself become the guide or even teacher, because its further "becoming processes" will be even formed in a language of your own specific recovery and discovery process. Each aspect of development in this corresponds to different areas of the brain in which new synapses begin to form and fusions of awareness begin to flower and bear fruit. The way in which certain brain areas work can become like pathways with which to conceive the world in more detail. Each part of the brain here can become a tool with which one can perceive the world better. Each area then is able to become a new form of comparison, developing with it a language that influences the perception over all other areas.

The Overall Intelligences, the Constant Dozen

Via the Empress and the "Intelligence of Desire," one develops a capacity to understand the world differently via processes that also exist during one's development of visualisation. With it, one learns to visualise things for better together with the realisation of a needed context of focus.

Via the Emperor or the "Loyal Intelligence," the talents will be developed via the hearing area (of the brain). Through the capacity of "hearing," this permits one to hear stages of development via what shows itself and also in their willingness to appear. One also hears to what degree people are committed and truly involved. One can hear the different goals and directions of people's desires by means of certain "intonations." This awareness does not depend simply on noticing other people's willingness but its reflection rather depends on one's own willingness to notice all the phases of involvement. By opening the mind further, one mobilises the ability to listen to what one does not yet know.

Via the High Priestess and the "Stable Intelligence," one develops a deeper awareness via the (brain) area of smell. With this awareness, one not only recognises the complexity of all stages of development but this time will also know how to combine certain stages (of developed awareness) so that one condition can more easily flow into the next. One can recognise stages of readiness and preparation.

Via Strength or the "Imaginative Intelligence," one develops an understanding of how to make connections via signals related with the (brain) region of speech. With its development, one starts to realise better how one can steer situations in this or that direction of development and how each will work practically. The area of speech corresponds with the area of impulses that steer one's behaviourism. It connects emotional involvement with rational preparation and instinctive reaction simultaneously.

Via Temperance or the "Intelligence of Temptation/Challenges," the truth of the saying "One becomes what one eats" will become more and more realised. This process of awareness develops itself by understanding more and more into detail in which one really connects or also commits oneself. Whatever commitments are made, and with it, elements added to the process, this will also include its own fit processes that demand an even greater commitment (of digestion) with which to realise interconnections before they can be fully integrated and become practical.

Via Love and the "Renewing Intelligence," one fuses the interactions between various levels of development of the senses so that all of them in their togetherness can be developed more fully. This is the stage where one realises the potentials of "group" energies. At this stage, one realises how certain combinations of persons can create stronger group energies with a higher exchange of talents, perspectives, and possibilities. Via certain combinations, certain developments simply grow in the direction of practical solutions and realisations much more quickly.

Via Justice or the "Natural Intelligence," one develops a sense of perspective directly via the practice of work itself. Work with and upon something will reveal through direct experience how things are done best.

Via the Wheel of Fortune or the "Tactile or Active Intelligence," one realises that through acting and adding more movement in accordance with the dance of events, the motor behind all activity is stimulated. This is about making opportunities, which always create such a form of stimulating energy that it further activates all commitment and puts into motion and into sight all the elements involved.

Via the (Falling) Tower or the "Physical Intelligence," one develops a sense for creating a direct effect upon all direct bodily reactions and develops a greater sense of people's instinctual behaviour via one's direct involvement. Thanks to this, no involved impulses are missed. They will all be steered along via further movement and involvement for the benefit of a common initiative. The physical intelligence controls the control centre over each initiative.

Via the Fool or the "Collective Intelligence," one learns to evaluate everyone's desire to become, and one learns to feel joy in their becoming. This phase is almost a synonym for the talent of one's general adaptation towards change, needed at each moment.

Via the Hermit or the "Ongoing/Continuing Intelligence," one learns to develop a sense of how to let things develop by themselves as things do in sleep. In this introverted stance, one learns to use a part of one's consciousness as though it were a kind of background "hum" via a mode of meditative awareness. This is like a constant dealing with, and being aware of, all the background changes of involvements towards what may appear at some stage.

Via Judgement or the "Assisting Intelligence," one learns to adapt to what is completely alien and unfit to interfere with, via an even further in the background lying process that can be compared to sleep. Thanks to the development of this area, one learns to deal with those aspects and waits patiently until some fit form emerges from it. At this stage, in all that is revealed or developed, a person learns at all times in balance with all the opposites and additional possibilities.

14

OVERVIEW

The Thirty-Third Path (111th or 0 Phase)

In the above diagram, we see represented the Triune World of the Three Arcana subdivided into six key divisions with Tao as centre. Previously, we saw how this centre split into two and gave rise to the Fool/Joker (right and left). This initial scission was followed by a division into three, incorporating the twenty-two cards of the Major Arcana (represented in our diagram by the light grey area, third ring from centre). The division into three was followed by a division into four, producing the four elements of the Minor Arcana, incorporating the fifty-six cards of the Royal Suits (represented by the four colours of the fourth ring). Following on from this, a further quintessential split divided the whole into five main areas (the largest area represented by the outer circle), consisting of the lower triangle, three connection points or spheres, and three neutral places for another twenty-two cards (in the dark grey area), while all other areas make associations with the four elements once again. Prior to this, the elements had just one point of connection in the Major Arcana. In the Third Arcana, however, there are one, two, three, or four points of connection. The Third Arcana (or outer circle in the above) taken separately and without the dark grey and neutralised region is again subdivided into five areas: two of which are combined into one, and another one is divided into two. All such links are interconnected. Within this entire structure, there is a harmoniously varying symmetry allied with an increasingly complementary asymmetry of detail. No system of five can be captured in a perfect symmetry. The quintessence is effective only when the elements are arranged according to their true meaning.

In this Grand Scheme, we have an overview of the entire system of cycles hidden within the tarot. All cycles possess three major stages: an initial starting point, a highlight, and an ending. In building up these thirty-two paths, we must take into account the operation of at least two levels simultaneously in each of the thirty-two phases. Each phase must be understood as being derived from a general stance or condition.

As regards the place of Truth and Intuition in the above scheme, it is important to stress once more that *The Fool's Tarot* subscribes neither to the order nor to the mode of approach expressed in *The Tarot of the Restored Order*, which conceives of Truth and Intuition as fully operational tarot cards. This is not how Truth and Intuition are to be understood in our system. As far as this work is concerned, these two Arcana have no influence on the traditional numbering of 21 + 1. This means we do not consider the Major Arcana as having twenty-four places. Instead, we can think of the two "extra places" as *directions* or directional indicators for thought.

One of these directions is represented by the large upper triangle, which originates from the small downward triangle representing Truth. The energy of Truth, which is *negative* in character, tends towards the earth and to a realisation of increased focus, which becomes more and more factual. It is "unfinished business," which requires working out further and which must complete itself before becoming fully mature or harmonic (neutral). The *red* colour, which this part eventually takes in the diagram, is the colour of such an aspect once it has been realised. In the thirty-third phase, it is fully achieved. Truth is then the complete cycle itself and no longer just the negative aspect that required recovery because something in the process had set off in the wrong direction because of an initial imbalance.

The opposite "direction" is the side that ought to be directly completed. Necessarily, this requires the correct "openness." It stands for the *positive* conditions and for Intuition. Relying on Intuition alone, however, cannot produce (or reshape) anything because the cycle would here stagnate. In practice, "openness" would find its neutrality much too soon. The concentration upon *neutral points* can only boost the cycle if the cycle itself does not become stagnant. Only Truth can recognise and name the stagnations caused by a cycle. Additional work and visions arising from Truth are necessary to provide balanced information before any final transformation can take place to complete the cycle.

Only at the end of the cycle—that is to say, in the thirty-third phase—will Intuition cease to be part of the process. When the entire cycle is completed, all intuitive elements become utilisable intelligences. Thus, the final result of the entire cycle is to reach the complete Truth in which Intuition is fully integrated as a *neutral agency*. In the process of completing the cycle, Intuition ought to become something of a supra-rational process (hence the colour *blue* in the diagram) and Truth something of a supra-emotional process (hence the colour *red* in the drawing). While Intuition initially occurred in a naturally sensitive and emotional manner, it becomes rational before being practical. In a similar vein, we can say of Truth that it must make contact with the higher emotional centre before it can really become practical. Too much "openness" leads to emotional chaos and a lack of rational discernment, whilst a plethora of disordered facts will affect the flow of emotional processes, making it impossible to find the necessary inspiration.

It is well to remember at this point that the theoretical abstract perspective of the overview contains a hidden Joker, who may spring forth at any moment with the admonition: *Now, discover your own practice!*

15

CONNECTING THE THREE ARCANA

To gain a clearer understanding of the scope, practical use, and distinct differences between the three Arcana, the following table has been devised:

<u>**The First Arcana**</u>	<u>**The Second Arcana**</u>	<u>**The Third Arcana**</u>
22 cards	56 cards	32 Intelligences
	Orientation of 4 stages	
General Attitudes		3 4 7 12
	 Cycle of Experience of 10	
	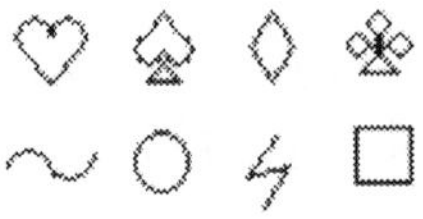	
	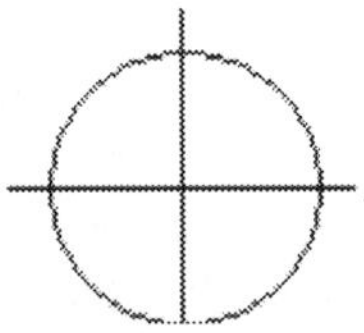 All cycles	
Realm of Desires	**Realm of Formation**	**Realm of Abstraction**

The full mandala here presented corresponds after a fashion to the model of the universe as found in the Hindu-Buddhist cosmology. This consists of three parts: Kãmadhãtu (the realm of desire), Rüpadhãtu (the realm of form), and Arüpadhãtu (the realm of formlessness). The Borobudur Temple in Java is divided according to this principle with three circles in the middle, starting with 4 x 4, or 16; followed by 4 x 6, or 24 (for 22 + 2); while the exterior is 4 x 8, or 32.

As mentioned earlier, the area of the First Arcana is associated with persons who are primarily guided by the automatism of their personalities. Such persons mechanically react to what their senses perceive and in the main use language as a means to articulate their basic desires. When this basic level of sensorial experience is deepened, a person has the possibility of passing beyond the state of dependency, to the level of the Second Arcana. Here, the person learns to shape their sensorial experiences by gradually gaining control over the four bodies of experience. These four bodies are summarised in the following table:

□ ♣	Earth	Clubs	harvesting	practice
∿ ♡	Water	Hearts	involvement	emotion
○ ♠	Air	Spades	"planting"	ratio
⚡ ◇	Fire	Diamonds	plowing field	instinct/ electricity

This evolution can best be understood by working from the bottom to the top. The first confrontation is largely instinctive and controlled by the processes of *attraction* and *repulsion*. Later, on the level of the Third Arcana, these confrontations will become a working area in which one learns to "steer" oneself. Whoever leads the process comes to certain rational conclusions about it. Whoever is drawn into the system experiences it in terms of emotional factors. Ultimately, a practical area exists that works best. The more formative field (the Second Arcana) depends on several cycles. Each process will initially be experienced through a conscious orientation in four stages. Each stage will unfold according to a particular pattern of ten Phases of Awareness.

For Readers wishing to draw cards under the auspices of a question concerning their own individual lives, it is important that consciousness of the process of becoming be fairly well developed. This is especially the case should they aspire to reach the level of the Third Arcana. At first, the Reader will find that it is only possible to perceive the familiar levels of the first two Arcana. After sufficient work and experience, however, a deepening of the relationship between the First and Second Arcana occurs. When this relationship is sufficiently advanced, the conditions for the transition from the Second to the Third Arcana are made possible. Whoever wishes to make the transition from the level of the Second Arcana to the level of the Third Arcana must take care to no longer act, think, or feel in a way that remains dependent on the processes operating at the level of the First Arcana.

At the point of transition, the sensitive Reader will immediately realise the value of the buffer zones Truth and Intuition. Those, on the other hand, who are still guided by the ego and by the impulses of power will remain dependent upon events. This in turn will cause their consciousness to be saturated by incomplete processes resulting in the blocking and obscuration of their intelligence. We might say that a prerequisite for entry into the Third Arcana—which makes possible the glorious opening up of perception that provides access to the inspiration of the Intelligences—is that all blocks and inhibitions contradicting the desired reality in which we live be removed.

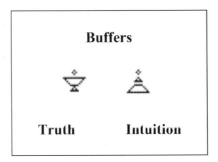

Buffers

Truth   **Intuition**

If one learns to handle Truth and Intuition, to navigate the buffer zones lying between the Second and the Third Arcana, noticing how experience and practice are connected in the process, one will then find that the mind is empty or free of pre-occupation and becomes open to inspiration moment to moment. Truth and Intuition then begin to work as "one entity." Intuition will be rapidly converted into intelligence and Truth laid upon the table as the articulation of all new material. In this arrangement, there is no longer any negative process (or negative energy). At this point, any and all confrontations encountered become beneficial. Thus, in the transition from the Second to the Third Arcana, any challenge or alleged offense that might occur whenever a certain element of truth is revealed can no longer harm one. When Truth and Intuition really do begin to work as one cooperating agency—which does not fully occur until all phases of the Third Arcana have been lived through and understood—the dualistic buffer zone of the First Arcana also becomes a gateway providing access from the First to the Third Arcana.

In relation to Reading Practices, consider the First Arcana as offering up a general layout or rough sketch of the situation. It is best to use the full eighty cards in becoming aware of all the processes involved. The *means of transition* from the Second to the Third Arcana are described by the initial ten paths of the thirty-two Paths of Wisdom. During these first ten phases, one learns to instinctively adapt better to all forms of inspiration. One begins to realise how a sound group mentality can be formed, maintained, and furthered, and also how important it is to maximise on the benefits of the impulses that are felt during its formation. But, of course, first, one must also learn to realise the nature of all impulses of processes that like to become, in the next three phases. Next, one learns to see how the impulses themselves evolve in nature and how they are truly balanced out during its whole process of formation, showing all of its practical and impractical aspects, until one learns to adapt oneself to it with full commitment while dealing with its inhabited nature of practicality. In the last twelve phases, one starts to mobilise also the understanding of one's own steering mechanisms and learns to notice what to deal with and how to develop one's senses better to each possible form of concretisation.

AFTERWORD: THE FOOL AS CENTRE OF PERCEPTION

It should be clear by now that the Fool is the one who undergoes All and Everything. The figure of the Fool is the common denominator of all the cards. In this sense, *everyone* is a Fool. The advantage of being a Fool is that via the Fool's "central nucleus of attention," one feels every impulse. However, under unfavourable conditions, a Fool becomes the victim of circumstance. We have seen that there are two extreme poles of the Fool: the ever-dependent or Zero-Point Fool (0), and the Consciously Adaptive or Total Fool (22). Between these poles stretches the full spectrum of human folly (the stances of the twenty-two types of Fool).

In his famous "Toasts to the Idiots," Gurdjieff used to goad his students: "Know the kind of Fool you are!" With this statement, Gurdjieff was clearly stressing the significance of knowing one's tendencies, one's inclinations, one's "chief feature" or major exaggeration. In every undertaking, one adopts this or that "stance," which, given the circumstances, may or may not be appropriate. In this respect, each role or mask that we assume may be experienced positively or negatively by others. One is generally only expected to emphasise or mobilise the "character" that suits a given person or situation (selecting one stance from twenty-two). Yet for all that, we tend to exaggerate our role up to twenty-one-fold. Given the likelihood that we only inhabit a situation properly and completely one time in twenty-two, it is perhaps not surprising that at all other times our behaviour is partially or even totally inappropriate (to the detriment of ourselves and others). Therefore, before mobilising oneself through the practices of this book, it is invaluable to ascertain the nature of one's own personal crystallisation. While *The Fool's Tarot* explains the theory of mobilisation or the activation of All and Everything, in practice, the ego strives to maintain various networks of obstruction. When this is the case, personality is stressed.

While astrology can be considered the art of learning to assess the ambient circumstances, *The Fool's Tarot* can be considered a complementary practice that aims to explore the attitudes or stances taken in relation to circumstances. Very often attitudes are much more determined *and* determining than the circumstances in which they occur. With this in mind, let us recall the attitudes we are likely to encounter, both in ourselves and in others, when we exaggerate the tendencies of the twenty-two degrees of folly.

The Twenty-Two Major Kinds of Fool

Whosoever exaggerates the role of the Fool will always and everywhere try to lose themselves in the circumstances that they encounter.

Whosoever exaggerates the role of the Magician will always and everywhere seek to manipulate people and circumstances to their own "perceived" advantage. This is done without any concern for the developmental needs of either.

Whosoever exaggerates the role of the Priestess cannot help but see the presence of the sublime and the mysterious in all circumstances. This is the figure of the "gypsy witch" who has become bewitched by the mists of her crystal gaze.

Whosoever exaggerates the Emperor will tend to patronise through an exaggerated display of paternal qualities. This is the "father figure" who cannot but take the lead in every enterprise.

Whosoever exaggerates the role of the Lovers will seek to conjoin with everyone in all circumstances. Such persons fail to understand other people's need for space and distance. They want to participate and to take part in everything to such a degree that their behaviour becomes irritating.

Whosoever exaggerates the role of the Priest can no longer participate naturally in anything anymore. Whether appropriate on all occasions, this person will translate everything into a message designed for the purposes of idealistic pontification.

Whosoever exaggerates the role of the Empress wants to nurture and take care of everyone at all times. This person always appears to be sitting on high extending their boundless beneficence with a self-satisfied sense of superiority. Such persons never (con)descend to "lower" themselves in the eyes of others (or themselves).

Whosoever exaggerates the role of the Chariot always and everywhere pursues victory and conquest. This person forever seeks to gain the upper hand even if this means sowing discord and destruction.

Whosoever exaggerates the role of the Hermit will withdraw to reflect at vital moments when circumstances require mobilisation and immediate action.

Whosoever exaggerates the role of Justice stands up for and defends the "rights" of various words and deeds at inopportune moments when the purveyor of the words or deeds in question should have been halted.

Whosoever exaggerates the role of Strength will emphasise power and become obsessed with the nature of power dynamics between persons and within circumstances.

Whosoever exaggerates the role of the Hanged Man tends to give in too easily because they look for circumstances greater than themselves. They would like to learn from all sorts of difficult situations but cannot tolerate the burden. Every move they mobilise is interpreted as a "necessary sacrifice." This leads to contradiction and to acting against one's own interests.

Whosoever exaggerates the tendencies of Temperance will always attempt to iron out the differences in every situation. Things are swiftly perceived as "out of balance" and in urgent need of redress. Such persons never take the opportunity to utilise imbalance to progress and change. Like the pedals of a bicycle deprived of the dynamics of alternation, the temperate fool suffers inertia.

Whosoever exaggerates Death will always emphasise what is not permitted and what cannot be done. The breach with the past remains a constant burden.

Whosoever exaggerates the tendencies of the Devil will always emphasise what binds or limits everyone and everything. This person cannot help but be a nasty critic.

Whosoever exaggerates the role of the Tower tends to dwell on the potential downfall of persons and situations. This person looks for circumstances that will challenge and topple the prevailing structure. Because of this, he always risks group exclusion.

Whosoever exaggerates the tendencies of the Moon overreacts emotionally to every event. For the lunar fool, such fluctuations seem to provide emotional depth. To everyone else, it looks like lunacy.

Whosoever exaggerates the Star is obsessed with fulfilling their own destiny and being recognised. These vain hopefuls view others as nothing more than pawns in their game.

Whosoever exaggerates the tendencies of the Sun will seek to illuminate and drag into the light those things that it is best not to be made aware of—that is to say, those things that still require time to gestate properly.

Whosoever exaggerates Judgement will always espouse an opinion on everything at all times and everywhere. Such persons fail to understand that there are many ideas and perceptions that are still in formation and require to be left alone rather than be assessed and pronounced upon.

Whosoever exaggerates the World considers only the world around them. Such fools give little or no attention to their own place within it.

When one knows one's dominant "inner tendency" (see above), one need not strive to alter this stance but rather to allow one's present "focus" to be supplemented by or to participate in all the other kinds of impulses so that all these aspects may assist in the development of a more complete picture of reality. One's own exaggerated tendency must gradually withdraw into the background somewhat in the manner of the Hermit, while other tendencies are accepted and validated in their participation. The emergence of these "Degrees of Folly" are always grounded in childhood experiences of deficiency and lack of integration, of unspoken complexes and retarded developments, rather than from a process of solid self-development. Perhaps more than anything else, the "Degrees of Folly" result from an excessive dependence on suspended processes.

Minor Roles

The Fool of "personal persuasion" is the Fool who lives and undergoes life as it appears while continuing in a particular role and experiencing all the drawbacks of a part that has failed to integrate with the whole. However, we must distinguish this Fool (0) from the essential Fool or Joker (22). The focus of an ordinary Fool, confined to a specific stance, tends to be crystallised in the moment. The Joker, on the other hand, tends to consider much larger time cycles such as, for example, those of the year. The perspective of "the moment" is determined by the freedom one is able to develop through the experience of the Major Arcana. This is influenced further by the different developmental stages of role playing that take place in the Minor Arcana: the mutual play of awareness (positive) and the termination of all its present aspects (negative).

Speaking in his work on *Natural Genesis*, Gerald Massey has this to say:

> The four Genii or gods of the four quarters, elements, colours, metals, etc., are also deposited in the pack of 52 playing cards. These are based on the four divisions of thirteen to the set, and the four: Ace, King, Queen, and Knave, preserve their places according to the latest arrangement in which the Sun-God is supreme. Harlequin is the Great One; the ruling power. The Ace takes all the tricks, just as Harlequin frustrates all the trickeries. The Ace is the Latin 'as', and in Egyptian 'as' means the Great One, the Supreme Ruler.

In Central Asia the game of chess which is believed to have had its origin in the Garden of Eden is played by four persons (instead of two as in modern practice) in keeping with the four quarters.[18]

Further on, Massey also mentions the roles or developmental attitudes of mother, child, adult, and old man as being four important phases in one's confrontation with life. More interesting from the point of view of this study and its relationship to the Fool are the four roles from the Italian *Commedia Harlequinade*, which actually display the four aspects of the Fool in the Minor Arcana. The four kinds of Fool or tendencies in life that play out the shadowy drama of the Second Arcana are represented by the characters *Columbine* (the indirect intellectual aspect engaging in reasoned tricks), the *Clown* (or Fool 0, representing one's current tendencies), the *Harlequin* (or Joker 22, the understanding presiding over what one is doing), and the *Pantaloon* (the direct action-oriented aspect—or sometimes Devil—engaging in the schemes and trickery of personal tendencies, often doing what he cannot resist from doing). In a more general sense, you can see these four key roles played out in the ordinary playing deck via the Queen (sensing), Knave (direct action or activity), Ace (understanding), and King (ruling).

Another example is to be found in the original game of chess with its sixty-four "places" or phases displaying the reality of change, played with 2 x 8 (16) figures and 8 supporting actors arranged in the form of a swastika. Here, the four figures are respectively an *elephant/unicorn* standing for the intellect (making a connection via fire); the *ship*, standing for the emotions (connected with water); the *horse*, representing the ego (via the earth); and the *king* or ether (related with language and the ear). It is not only the players who control the game but also the dice, which determine destiny and emphasise the dependency of everyone's role.[19]

Here, once again, it becomes clear that the Great Game must be played and that the different angles—always a minimum of four—are necessary to achieve a vision over events via perception through the four senses and the four bodies of experience. Complete observation from the four centres or bodies of experience is made through the ten phases of preparation, which combine to create a unity of perception allowing for a balanced vision of the presenting elements.

The Third Arcana: The Initiator

The Third Arcana has been described via the role of the Joker and the role of the Fool, who has the choice of whether to respond to all his impulses. He who takes account of every impulse will become part of All and Everything. It is useful in life to integrate each impulse, each message, and to integrate everyone's role in the development of the Whole. This path corresponds with Gurdjieff's Fourth Way.

---

[18] Massey, Gerald (Natural Genesis vol. 1), pp. 414–416.
[19] See Egbert Richter-Ushanas (The Indus Script and the Rig-Veda, Motilal Banarsidass Publications, Delhi, 1997–2001).

Appendix 1

ATTRIBUTION OF THE FOUR ELEMENTS TO THE FOUR TAROT SUITS

It is to be noted that some interpreters attribute the suit of clubs to the element earth, while others attribute diamonds to this same element. Again, some interpreters attribute spades to the element water, while others attribute the suit of hearts to the element fire, which cannot be true. First of all, the suits themselves do not actually represent the elements but rather represent *our relationship* to the elements. Second, the suit of diamonds at first glance looks like an earth square—that is to say, a productive field. However, the diamond is related more to our intention to labour in the earth, which is more properly a function of the fire element derived from the act of fertilisation—which could eventually relate to the element of air and so on. Hearts are also driven by a certain fire—or is it warmth?—(but not by heat) and also by water, emotions. Spades can stand for the intellect, which can also be likened to the creative inspiration of fire. In terms of *The Fool's Tarot*, of course, the phases concerned with the suit of spades refer only to the rational processes represented by air and which work best under the element of air. Although different attributions can be taken in laying a foundation, the most important factor to bear in mind are the relationships of the elements with human experience and the evolutionary cycles of creation.

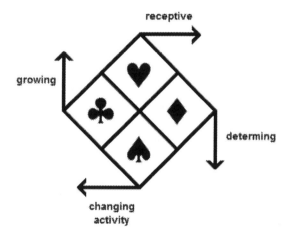

For a spontaneous evolutional path in the course of life and in the order as it occurs most frequently, see the order indicated above. These are "fixed rules of change," which occur on the level of the Second Arcana and can be associated as spontaneously occurring processes within the circumstances of the four seasons: beginning with practical growth in spring, a sensitive perception in summer, determining choices and confrontations in harvest, and a rational mobility in winter.

Appendix 2

INNER MOBILITY OF THE FOUR CENTRES OF EXPERIENCE

We can compare the four bodies or centres of experience with the theosophical system of four sensory vehicles: causal body, mental body, astral body, and physical body. These four vehicles are too often imagined as real bodies each with their own separate and distinct kind of material. While one might expect that the causal body would correspond with the confrontational centre, the latter is in fact comparable to a form of "astral" sensitivity that includes impulses from the physical, emotional, and mental levels. Moreover, in theosophical circles, a distinction is often made between higher and lower mental impulses, which can be very confusing. In *The Fool's Tarot*, the choice was made not to use impractical terms such as "higher consciousness" because of the vagueness of such terminology and the danger of associating these kinds of simplistic notions with all manner of projections. Understanding the "abstract world," however, may involve a separate source of inspiration and a totally different context that has nothing to do with an increase in rational processing. Indeed, its underlying source of inspiration and even understanding need not be a "mental" one at all. Which context it could have should have become somewhat clearer through this work.

To explain how the four bodies of experience fit with the Minor Arcana and which degree of emphasis they have in the creative processes related to the other Arcana is expressed in the following diagram:

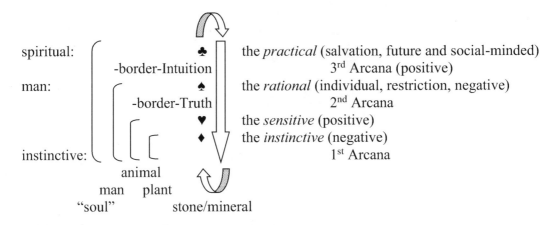

In the above diagram, the arrows reveal how the development of one process will trigger another. None of these processes actually run separately. For example, when the rational mind learns to work in a more intuitive way, this will, in turn, start to influence the instinctive part. An intuitive mind will only become like a higher form of intellect—with additional features— once it has developed the more practical side within it. Only such a "higher mind" can use hidden intelligences to form instinctive directives so that it can pass through the right incentives in an increasingly more and more automated process. These elements together feed it on different planes simultaneously. The conclusions and talents one thereby develops are also directed from the practical side of the nature to track down its own element as a self-renewing impulse. Rationality alone is incapable of coming to that.

Another diagram that shows how consciousness may develop within these four bodies of experience can be seen below:

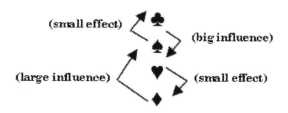

where
- the *instinctive* "fires"/sparks the mind (= great influence)
- the *ratio* makes things practical (= with small effect)
- the *practical* provokes feelings (= great influence)
- the *feelings* tend to steer the instinctive (= with small effect)
- and this *instinct* makes confrontation with the mind (= great
    influence) by which
- the *ratio* reacts to this confrontation, and so on . . .

Appendix 3

THREE COORDINATING FUNCTIONS, THREE DYNAMICS, THREE ARCANA, THREE TYPES

Each system with a process of evolution meant to create awareness can be approached in three different ways. Each of these approaches gives different actions and reactions and reveals in fact different goals of stress upon the system.

Some approaches do not take us much further. For what concerns the comparison of the Kabbalistic Tree of Life with the thirty-two parts, some people just simply count the numbers of the Sephiroth and then add extra numbers to the paths, something that leads to rather irrelevant associations.

Other approaches show us rather weak forces of dynamics in the system. When we, for instance, take the three paths 11,12, and 13 to analyse further "the perfect 3," which are related with the three main and most important coordinating functions in the system, in the order of the thirty-two cards by Rawn Clark, the centres in his system are not Devil (15), Magician (1), World (22), and a fourth centre describing the neutralising factor, the Chariot (8), but instead are Temperance (13), High Priestess (2), and Ordeal (20). Together, in this sort of combination of centres, this seems at first sight something more like a tempered (so in this case, like a secondary) ordeal taken from a wider, less involved distance, without much participation of the inner activation of any of the potentials that could be activated on any of the parts. Nevertheless, I will, further on, be able to show how these centres will still reveal something like an accompanying low-profile side effect in its process.

The dynamics of a recovery system need a dependence on a much more active process of balancing out of circumstances. Such a balance, in realty, is much more governed just like the pulling of strings between one maximum (22 aspects) and one minimum (0 aspects) of unfolding potentials, of which the 0-centre of movement is governed by a system of circumstances. Drawn upon a circle, this process of becoming turns to the right, further into its natural cause and growth process. The forces upon the Now (symbolised by 1, as the actual and factually started engagement, with man experiencing it all) are revealing itself like forces of a wave pushed upwards and downwards in a rhythm according to the amount of elements involved. Its balancing forces shows its effects in the Fool. The whole system of dynamics with twenty-two places I will draw further on with the help of three double triangles of six, while the dynamic system remains between two opposites of Fool, with one centre of focus of a chosen reality, the Magician, which process will show itself in a sevenfold inner evolution, giving it a personal evolutionary workout.

According to the stress on the system, the traditional system of thirty-two parts shows us the centres 1 for Magician, 8 for Strength, and 22 for Fool. These sorts of at each stage neutralised centres in this system are the guides in which a certain balance and neutral reality and material is found in each stage, where they belong. These centres show the most obvious and also most automatic to follow guides or guidelines for one's personal evolution plan and path from which one already knows by now that one ought to follow in this process of becoming and realisation or in realising something in the world. Within this process of becoming, one should realise by now also that the Fool rules one's own awareness in the life stream via the realisations of its direct effects upon oneself. Via the centre of Strength (needed especially when one would like to add more material into the process), there remains a personal control over one's own direct actions. Within this active system, one could still stress emphasis onto what tensions are felt directly into its own potential (0-governed) or what effect is given onto the feedback system itself (22).

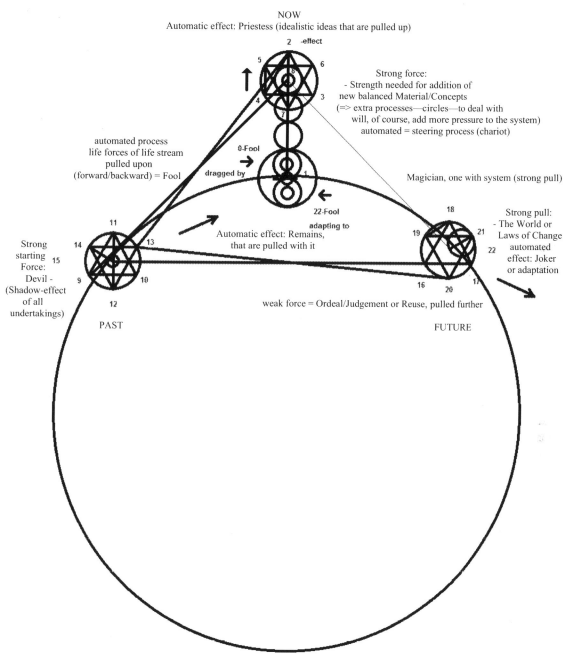

The dynamic "motor" system,
showing the passive tensions of dynamics and the active tensions of formation

By describing also the differences in this awareness process between the strong effects and the weak forces that guide the process together with the already known three dynamic coordinating functions, one will learn that at each moment one can chose to participate with the weak or strong forces as well. These choices will fit with the aforementioned types or attitudes of participants at each moment of the process (the type that does not want to participate, the type that wants to experience, and the type that wants to restore the situation).

Two different forces come from the past. Death is the weak force that is automatically leftover from the past. This is what comes along as the remains, without forcing itself into the system. The Devil, however, is the strong force from the past, which is the energy that is pulled back from all the shadow effects from unfinished businesses. It is the purpose of recovery to integrate this back into the system and will also force itself that way.

A strong bi-effect upon the Now is, of course, Strength, which is the true accompanying force that takes care that someone has the courage to add even more material into the process. The neutralised strong force is, of course, the Chariot or steering force itself, with which one still could mobilise each moment, if one would like to use this for what it may mean, its involvement in how much one would like to neutralise each involved element. This driving force to add material is one's own power and freedom to decide in which direction one would like to go at each moment. A weak force but still an inspiration is the amount of idealism that will decide the process (Priestess). Be reminded that it is not the ambition and the talent that will develop itself here but, in the first place, the accompanying force to steer competently.

The strongest pull towards the future is the World, which will decide what it will do not only with all your ambitions but also with your form of steering. All this will give a strong effect upon the Joker. A weak side effect of this will be the amount of material that will be reused.

In this process, we have not only strong pulls but also effects and side effects. Here, we can already recognise ideas that we will be able to use to understand later the general dynamics of change. This dynamic system of pulling of the strings with its three sorts of pulling strings in the system, also known by the name of Tensegrity, will be further explained in volume 2.

It is true that in this last scheme, the Magician seems to be the stable force; in reality, the conclusion of stress upon the Magician is only due to the results it is able to describe and articulate, while the real processes are gathered and experienced in the two Fools automatically. The stress of awareness over these felt effects can be pulled either towards a certain backward move, back towards its centre of innocence, with the 0-Fool, realising mostly only its inhibited process, with less influence even from its own interference (1), or it will rather focus even more forward as the Joker (22), a move towards the stretching of its own limits and further unfolding of possibilities, with more general activation in and from all processes.

In its learning process, one can chose and mainly seek stabilisation and balance. With its ruler of awareness, Fool 0, this approach fits best with the Major Arcana. This is related with the first type of participants (i.e., those who seek a low profile). This type of people remains dependent on the processes themselves in which they will be confronted and forced to change by the elements of its own inner structure alone. This is the slowest and most dependent process of progress. One could also focus on discovering its limits, with the Fool 22 in its centre of awareness (via the minor arcana). But one could also engage willingly in a recovery process. Here, one must learn to become *one* with the purpose of becoming, also expressed in the three coordinating principles. In its follow-up, the Fool finally steps forward as a Magician.

The message to be learned from facing the different stresses you take in the system is clear and can be taken to the interpretation of a reading (past/present/future):

- Be cautious about everything from the past, because it is incomplete, and what you notice is a shadow of existence that still needs to become complete.

- Note that you are the one who is able to make things clear. It is that kind of steering of the material that will give things a new purpose.
- It still is up to the World to decide what will be effective or not and which clarification is satisfying.

People of low profile do not engage the incompleteness of what is revealed or will not help to reveal further the shadow of things. For them, they only are left with dead remains. They still idealise their talents and vision, are dependent like fools, but still think they are in control, but will mostly confirm a certain annoying repetitive tendency. All they contribute will sooner or later be judged upon whether it will get another chance to be reused again and again. In reality, what needs to change still cannot, because the poorly expressed elements in their order will always remain inferior. Such people need the teacher. As explained in chapter 9, the teacher will emphasise a powerful stress upon the system so that each "becoming" truly is mobilised.

For the sake of improvement, a person who wants to integrate in life always needs to be guided (in dependence, Fool) and not guide everything himself like the Magician. So it is more useful to be as normal and modest as possible, depending on the needs of this guiding process, to make all necessary changes or continuations possible. The only thing people can mobilise as "talents" in an active form is to follow the true necessity, which is in fact at each moment the real minimum one can do. When you can discover yourself, it can become your own language of a necessity, leading the process with it, not under the form of a process of maintaining something, and not to survive but really while being engaged in a process with the purpose to add life, adding exactly what had been a shadow before and was realised as such.

The leading figure in a process, for this purpose, obviously needs to take the role of a teacher (guru, leader of a project) in times of blockages and sometimes needs to strike a blow of seemingly aggressive contra-response, via an energy of negativity, striking it towards especially the persons who represent the first type who no longer want to participate in renewal, and who will only take a distance, rationalising their ideas of non-movement as if they are the ones who need to stand firm and strong and decisive in their nature, like "leaders" under control of it all, in self-protection; in reality, at those stages, they are also too stubborn and not prepared to change along with the process in need. The energy that at such stages is felt as being negative includes in fact also their own Devil in disguise, which in combination with the teacher's force, like that towards the Hanged Man forcing him from the Ivory Tower, will show someone with a stronger force of suggestion, the need to face unknown realisations. The passive man, however, in such situations will always rather prefer almost religious types of rather positive suggestion, for which he will remain with his ideas in the passive states of Temperance (13), while being inspired only by his own ambitions, High Priestess (2), and will leave the final effects to what happens automatically long time afterwards, in the Ordeal. This is the slow path in which such a person who stops the matters for the leading people will need to step down from the participating responsibilities, because with it, no leadership of events will be able to be activated much further.

In activities where there exists little communication, the kind of slow process (and progress) always plays in the background constantly, like a process of awaiting feedback. This is able to continue slowly as long as the joint forces still are involved in all that can be revealed and transformed in the final and most active form of this process. The strongest progress itself is always the most direct one, demanding in its result immediate change out of necessity. In processes where there is little communication, however, the slow feedback process of the last ordeal will be more permanent and dependent. The leader of a project can show at times more immediate negative remarks and with it will distinguish who will pass for further responsibility or who in the end will not.

Just in case, people, in their religious interpretations, would start to call the past "diabolical" in an erroneous interpretation of the matters above, as what had been described above. I will explain this once more differently: the Devil here as the past means that all that you can activate can only be a shadow of itself; otherwise, it will be a passive or a neutral residue. Either you watch those remains (Death) or you are able to reactivate life in it via the understanding of its lack of life and its negative conditions where it cannot add full life. In such a process, thanks to better and further articulations of what it really could be, for its completion and contribution to life itself, one understands and rediscovers certain missing elements from it in the present, feeling from it, what life it truly is able to bring into the Now. Only then it can really be given to the world for its true effects, which is a Future.

Also, these people, using religion as an excuse to hide their own shadows, think they need to stand strongly against temptation, against "evil" that they place on the outside,[20] as if avoiding their own participation or responsibility of choice; in that way, the Ordeal over it is cancelled towards an endless delay of the process, until the "end of time." What is also needed here is a better articulation of one's own participation in the direct communicative process that receives its most honest responses directly in the World. Giving the world a real future depends on the willing, to be fully engaged in the process (the Second Arcana), being ready and prepared to participate also in every form of feedback (the Third Arcana), being a part of participation.

---

[20] I blame this on the incorrect translation of the Bible, where Jesus is in the desert. In fact, he didn't say to Satan, "Go away," but rather, "Follow Me," something the translators did not know how to interpret or how to fit this into their ideas and verify their rational. Nevertheless, it isn't so weird for the shadow that it must follow the light. Simply because of this wrong interpretation, people who were different were persecuted, while one's own sins were leftover to a confession to a priest, and a real confrontation from dealing with this was delayed until the Last Ordeal. This Ordeal, which even during a year's cycle of events could come much sooner, is preferably delayed until the end of an era of such a group-based thought processes. Such a group will only start its own evolution of transformations sooner via individual liberations. The different learning processes useful for a Christian context as well as other further guiding methods will be explained in volume 2.

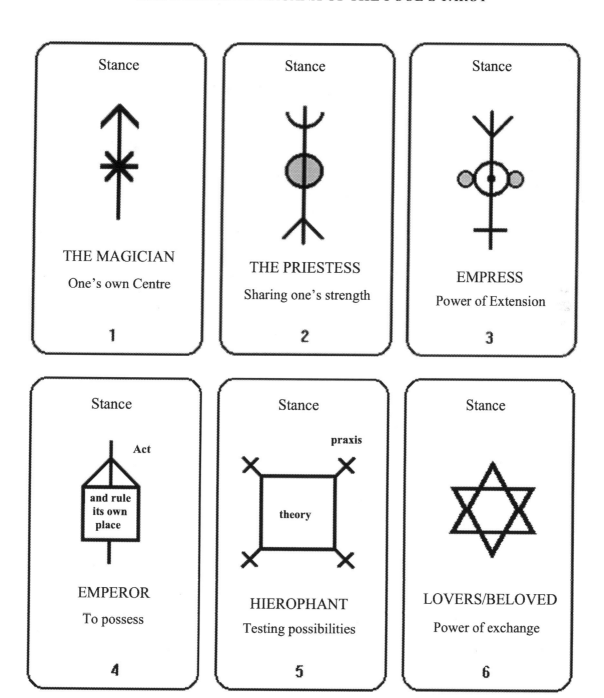

Stance

THE MAGICIAN

One's own Centre

1

Stance

THE PRIESTESS

Sharing one's strength

2

Stance

EMPRESS

Power of Extension

3

Stance

Act

and rule
its own
place

EMPEROR

To possess

4

Stance

praxis

theory

HIEROPHANT

Testing possibilities

5

Stance

LOVERS/BELOVED

Power of exchange

6

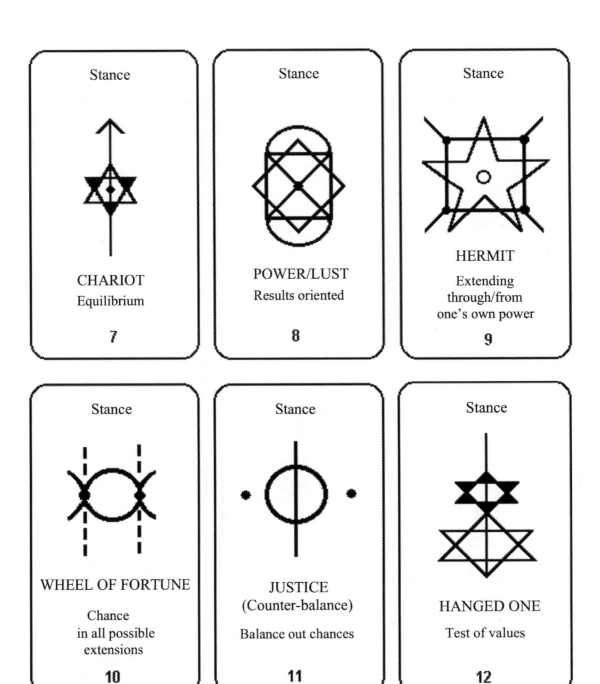

Stance

CHARIOT
Equilibrium

7

Stance

POWER/LUST
Results oriented

8

Stance

HERMIT
Extending
through/from
one's own power

9

Stance

WHEEL OF FORTUNE

Chance
in all possible
extensions

10

Stance

JUSTICE
(Counter-balance)

Balance out chances

11

Stance

HANGED ONE
Test of values

12

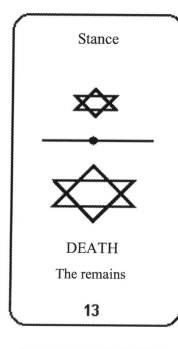

DEATH

The remains

13

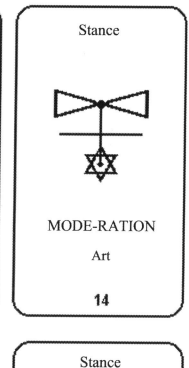

MODE-RATION

Art

14

DEVIL

The shadow side
of one's own power
begins to unfold

15

FALLING TOWER

A test case for
what one puts one's energy
or commitment into

16

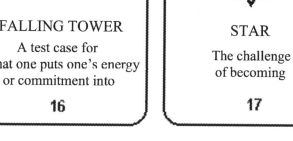

STAR

The challenge
of becoming

17

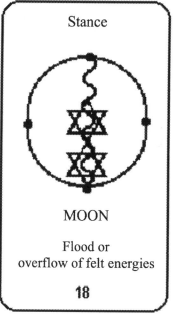

MOON

Flood or
overflow of felt energies

18

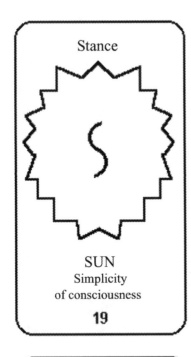

Stance

SUN

Simplicity
of consciousness

19

Stance

JUDGEMENT/AEON

A re-use

20

Stance

WORLD/UNIVERSE

Knowing one's place

21

Stance

FOOL/JESTER/JOKER

The naïve

22

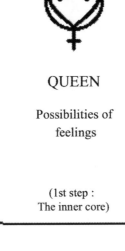

Hearts ♡ Cups

QUEEN

Possibilities of
feelings

(1st step :
The inner core)

Hearts ♡ Cups

KING / PRINCE

Directed feelings:

Desire

(2nd step: "in volume")

Hearts ♡ Cups

KNIGHT

The Totality
of feelings:

Locomotion

(3rd step: whole)

Hearts ♡ Cups

PRINCESS / PAGE

The Unity
that makes feelings

(4th step: on the outer edges)

Hearts ♡ Cups

ACE
(Axe)

Meaning of life

1

Hearts ♡ Cups

LOVE

Feelings to share

2

Hearts ♡ Cups

ABUNDANCE

Voice of the Heart

3

Hearts ♡ Cups

WEALTH

Where feelings go

4

Hearts ♡ Cups

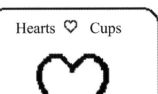

DISAPPOINTMENT

Feelings with a place
outside the heart

5

Hearts ♡ Cups

JOY / BLISS

Productive grounding

6

Hearts ♡ Cups

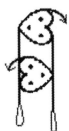

FEELINGS ENHANCED
NO LONGER IN
CONTROL

Corruption

7

Hearts ♡ Cups

to carry

to bear

ENDURABLE/
BEARABLE

To carry (on)
an attitude

8

Hearts ♡ Cups

GLADNESS /
CONTENTMENT

Spreading out
feelings

9

Hearts ♡ Cups

FULLNESS

The complete package
of feelings

10

Swords ♠ Thoughts	Swords ♠ Thoughts	Swords ♠ Thoughts

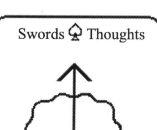

QUEEN

Starting to grasp
the 'other' side

1st step

KING/PRINCE

See the
joint / shared
possibilities

2nd step

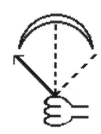

KNIGHT

clinching insight &
givers of strength

3rd step

Swords ♠ Thoughts	Swords ♠ Thoughts	Swords ♠ Thoughts

PAGE / PRINCESS

The Weapon
of the Mind:

direct(ion)
by enlightening &
making 〔 〕 lighter

4th step

ACE/AXE

Self-recognition

1

PEACE

evaluating directions

2

Swords ♠ Thoughts	Swords ♠ Thoughts	Swords ♠ Thoughts

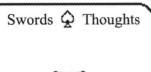

DOOM & GLOOM

Locked up

3

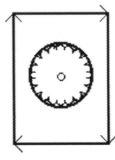

PEACE OF ARMS

Round Table
unity

4

DEFEAT

Oppression
caused by
weaknesses

5

Swords ♠ Thoughts	Swords ♠ Thoughts	Swords ♠ Thoughts

SCIENCE

Comparison
on the foundations
of changes

6

FUTILITY

Contradictions,
deceit, forgiveness
Counter-arguments
become arguments

7

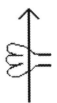

INTERFERENCE

Accepting an
inability

8

Swords ♠ Thoughts

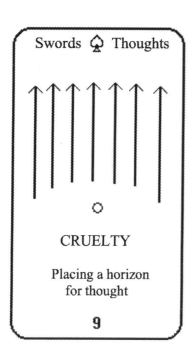

CRUELTY

Placing a horizon
for thought

9

Swords ♠ Thoughts

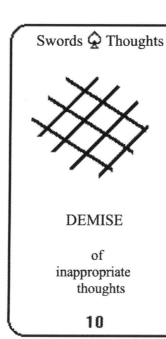

DEMISE

of
inappropriate
thoughts

10

Clubs ♣ Pentacles
Results

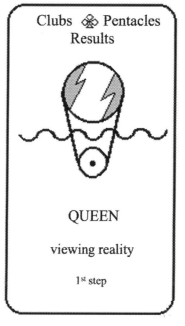

QUEEN

viewing reality

1st step

Clubs ♣ Pentacles
Results

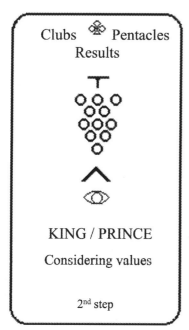

KING / PRINCE

Considering values

2nd step

Clubs ♣ Pentacles
Results

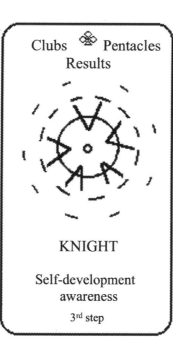

KNIGHT

Self-development
awareness

3rd step

Clubs ♣ Pentacles
Results

PRINCESS / PAGE

Check the
unfolding
opportunities

4th step

Coins 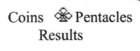 Pentacles Results	Coins  Pentacles Results	Coins Pentacles Results

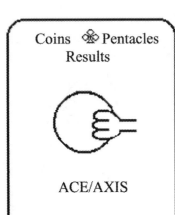

ACE/AXIS

Talents
and
potential forces

1

**(EX)CHANGE
OR
REPETITION**

2

WORK / LABOUR

3

**BACKUP/
PACKAGE**

Collecting facts

4

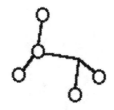

**TORMENT
WORRIES**

by weak consistency

5

SUCCESS

productive
coherence

6

Coins 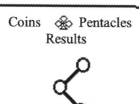 Pentacles
Results

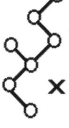

FAILURE

due to measure
or time-dependent coherence

-immaturity-

7

Coins Pentacles
Results

CAUTIOUSNESS

knowing patterns
for creating fruitful result

8

Coins Pentacles
Results

PROFIT

Harvest
within a location

9

Coins 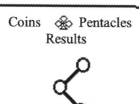 Pentacles

WEALTH

Tree of Life:
full sum of possibilities

10

Wands ◊

QUEEN

1st preparation:
Testing the foundations

Wands ◊

KING / PRINCE

2nd preparation:
Distribute the testings

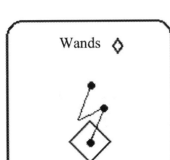

Wands ◊

KNIGHT

3rd preparation:
Directing
the assignments

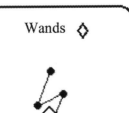

Wands ◊

PRINCESS / PAGE

4th step:
Engaging enthusiasm

Wands ◊

ACE/ AXE

giving direction
to the ordeals / trials

1

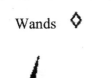

Wands ◊

DOMINION

Orientation for
the direction
of assignments

2

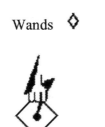

Wands ◊

**MAKING A
VIRTUE OF NEED**

3

Wands ◊

REPLENISHMENT

uniting activities

4

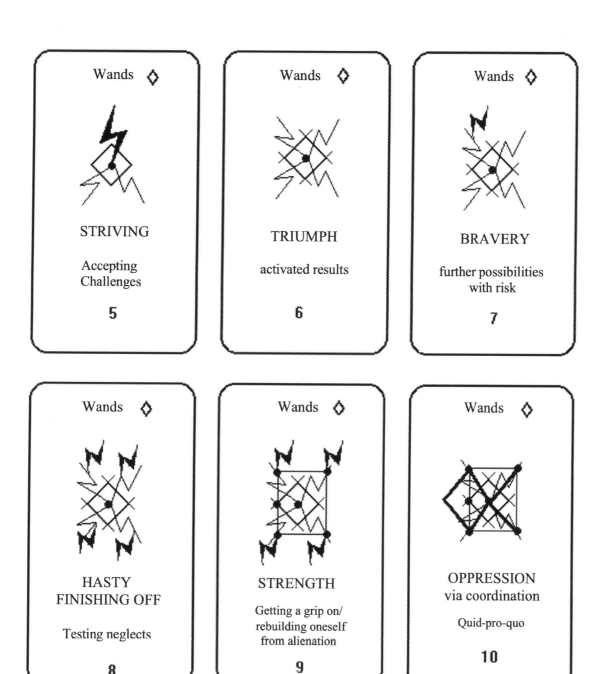

Wands ◊

STRIVING

Accepting
Challenges

5

Wands ◊

TRIUMPH

activated results

6

Wands ◊

BRAVERY

further possibilities
with risk

7

Wands ◊

HASTY
FINISHING OFF

Testing neglects

8

Wands ◊

STRENGTH

Getting a grip on/
rebuilding oneself
from alienation

9

Wands ◊

OPPRESSION
via coordination

Quid-pro-quo

10

OPEN PLACE FOR

INTUITION

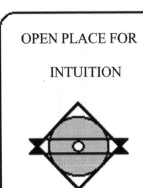

(increasing volume)

complement
the missing parts

WORKING AREA OF

TRUTH

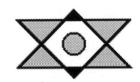

(confirm the centre,
strengthen one's edges)

placing/protecting the known

- - < + - -

Printed in the United States
by Baker & Taylor Publisher Services